The Miracle of The Mysteries

Revealed through the Hearts Secrets

By
Carmel Glenane B.A. Dip. Ed.

The Miracle of The Mysteries

Revealed through the Hearts Secrets

By
Carmel Glenane B.A. Dip. Ed.

Big Country Publishing, LLC

The Miracle of The Mysteries, Revealed through the Hearts Secrets
©2016 by Carmel Glenane B.A. Dip. Ed.
ISBN: (print) 978-1-938487-27-9
ISBN: 978-1-938487-28-6 (eBook)
Library of Congress Control Number: 2016941012
Cover background image: 59790807 ©Sakkmesterke Dreamstime.com

All rights reserved. No part of this publication may be reproduced, stored in a retrieval system, or transmitted, in any form or by any means electronic, mechanical, photocopying, recording, or otherwise without prior written permission from the publisher except in the case of brief quotations embodied in critical articles and reviews.

The author and publisher of the book do not make any claim or guarantee for any physical, mental, emotional, spiritual, or financial result. All products, services, and information provided by the author are for general education and entertainment purposes only. The information provided herein is in no way a substitute for medical or other professional advice. In the event you use any of the information contained in this book for yourself, the authors and publisher assume no responsibility for your actions. Big Country Publishing, LLC accepts no responsibility or liability for any content, bibliographic references, artwork, or works cited contained in this book.

Published by Big Country Publishing, LLC 7691 Shaffer Parkway, Suite C, Littleton, CO 80127 USA www.bigcountrypublishing.com
Printed in the United States of America, United Kingdom, and Australia
Books may be ordered through the publisher for wholesale, booksellers or by contacting:
Atlantis Rising Healing Center
P.O. Box 376, Coolangatta, QLD, 4225 Australia
+61 (0) 7 55 367 399
www.carmelglenane.com
www.atlantis-rising.com.au
www.senjukannonreiki.com

Because of the dynamic nature of the Internet, any web addresses or links contained in this book may have changed since publication and may no longer be valid.

Table of Contents:

Acknowledgements 7
Preface 9

Part I: The Divine Feminine Mysteries 11
The Secret Garden Visualization 17
Adventure of Self Discovery Visualization 20
The Scarab Visualization 24
Visualization for Accessing Sound 26
Pacha Mama's Story 28
Surrender Visualization 30
Assembling the Jig Saw of Being Human 31
The Spider – "Aracne's" Visualization 34
Visualization – The Sphinx 42
The Breath of Creation Visualization 45
Bliss Visualization 48
Release Visualization 51
Entering through the Gates 52
The Red Room Visualization 60
The Red Room and Serpent Visualization 63
Anubis Meditation 89

The Keepers of The Mysteries of the
Divine Feminine Meditation 90

Part II: Entering the Portal of the Heart's Secrets 93
The Heart's Secrets 94
The Five Bodies 113
The First Law: Stillness 130
The Second Law: Balance 131
The Third Law: Frequency 133

Bibliography 135
About the Author 137
Meditations by Carmel Glenane 139
Other Books by Carmel Glenane 143
Tours and Events with Carmel Glenane 151

Acknowledgement

The Keepers of The Mysteries of the Divine Feminine

This transmission is dedicated to all Light workers who have enabled me to co-create with The Keepers

Preface

The first part of this book was born on an early morning in Luxor, Egypt on the top deck of a cruise ship, where our Great Mother, the Nile, rocked us as we anchored the Divine Feminine Mysteries through group meditation on this spiritual teaching journey. On the Grand Quintile, October 28, 2004, where the moon was in eclipse Taurus/Scorpio, I led a meditation and held space for my students to Earth the Divine Feminine Mysteries. I thank all of the students on this tour for their dedication in being pioneers; anchoring the Divine Feminine Mysteries here on Earth.

Eleven years later, on June 21, 2015, in Piedris Nigras, Mexico, this book was given to "The Mayan Masters of Light" in this ancient site. In a ceremony led by Miguel Angel Vergara, a Mayan priest and teacher living in Yucatan, and Trudy Woodcock, a Mayan High Priestess, where I participated in a powerful ceremony on a tour to access "The Akashic Records."

This book completes a series of books beginning with "The Alchemies of Isis Embodiment through The High Priestess." The body of work is a step-by-step journey into the pure intelligence of your heart's truth, bringing a connection to your heart you could never have previously imagined. You have now in your hands and in your heart, your own blue print for yourself to step into the brave new frontier of "Self Responsibility" by listening to your "Secret Heart" through The Miracle of The Mysteries.

Part One:

The Divine Feminine Mysteries

What are the Divine Feminine Mysteries?

The Mysteries of the Divine Feminine consciousness is a belief in the immortality of the soul, i.e. The soul is a separate individual entity that sets to forward its truth by incarnating in a human body. The soul seeks to draw on past incarnations in this vehicle, the body, and find balance in the act of loving the self. The soul struggles with this most of the time, because the decision was made in a state of purity and extreme bliss; however the soul challenges itself to seek to find this self love through the journey of being human. As the soul is immortal and timeless, its journey in being human is naturally fraught with perils through its many incarnations on Earth. The Mysteries of the Divine Feminine gives this soul a chance to experience immortality on Earth by drawing on the ancient wisdom of self nurturing, through enacting The Mysteries here on Earth, and having a parallel reality on Earth, in its temporal state, while experiencing the state of transcendence in being human.

This book draws on the ancient wisdom of the principle of self-nurturing and will outline in an easy step-by-step format the recipe for drawing on these Mysteries. Mysteries are just that, they are mysteries until revealed. The soul is thirsty to seek the old Mysteries once again to make the journey an experience it originally intended, the original intention being "self" love.

To understand the "Miracle of The Mysteries" is to feel that you are in the presence of those who hold The Mysteries. The beings that presented themselves as those who hold The Mysteries are called *The Keepers of The Mysteries.*

Visualize who The Keepers of The Mysteries could be, and why you seek The Mysteries of the Divine Feminine, which is the principle of self-nurturing.

Let's begin to meet "The Keepers."

You will need sacred oil to anoint yourself (rose oil is beautiful).

Now, allow yourself to be in the presence of The Keepers of The Mysteries.

Just feel the soft, gentle presence of yourself. You need to feel this soft, melting, receptive energy emanating from you to magnetize The Keepers of The Mysteries to you.

Your breath is essential and so is stillness; combine the breath with the stillness now.

Breath is the only way you will draw a spiritual vibration to you.

Breathe in slowly, rhythmically and powerfully. There are many breath techniques.

For now, allow yourself deep rhythmic breathing. Just keep drawing in the breath, slowly, powerfully and rhythmically. Feel the soft hypnotic effect of the breath. This state must be achieved before you begin to feel the presence of The Keepers of The Mysteries.

Begin now to gently sway or rock to the rhythm of the breath.

Do this now, and do this for as long as you need to. Just be in the loving presence of the breath as you rock and sway.

Now bring the breath to your heart and breathe into your heart center, seeing the heart open wide now to receive the message from The Keepers of The Mysteries.

You may like to practice this now, and allow yourself to feel peace-filled.

Feel this peace now.
1) Anoint yourself
2) Allow yourself to receive
3) Breathe deeply, powerfully, rhythmically
4) Rock gently
5) Go to your heart center

As you melt into your heart center try to imagine The Keepers as storytellers, reading an ancient, long-forgotten script to you.

The story of creation is one of mystery; in fact, mystery surrounds all of creation, and it is to our own creation we must turn toward to enact The Mysteries of old. Our creation is a mystery in so much as it is really unknown to our other self, our self that lives in everyday reality. It is therefore essential that we turn off the light switch that continually re-enforces our mortal self and not our mysterious self. Our mysterious self is the code-breaker to free the mortal self to experience living not only as a human but also humanely to the self.

Reflect on this story and breathe its message into your heart center.

Mystery always implies fear, danger and adventure rolled into one. Our primitive brain usually reacts to mystery with terror. A fear is immediately established, and our primitive brain shuts down. There is an instant frozen moment, where the joy of what may have been mysterious, a revelation, is not allowed to be accessed. The primitive brain has control and the mystery of being human, the mystery of the potential creative self, is gone forever in some cases, and "you" the human, walk around with "blinkers" on, never knowing just why you are here, and why you don't believe that "a pot of gold" at the end of the rainbow could ever exist.

There is a pot of gold at the end of the rainbow. The imagination wants to believe in the mystery.

The logical mind says: *"Nonsense, how can this be, it is stupid, fanciful and childish. Stop this silly imagining; this talk is only for children and imbeciles. Stop it now."*

So, over time, the imagination stops and The Mysteries, the secrets of the Divinely Feminine ones cannot be accessed at all. The facility for this imagination is lost forever in some cases.

Bringing The Mysteries into your consciousness creates commitment to a view of reality others may not share with you, and now is a time to make a decision as to how you will live your life free of other's attachments to you. Admittance to The Mysteries requires separateness; separation from those who may not tolerate your "expanded" view of consciousness. Yet this is all it is, an "expanded" view of consciousness. Your lens is wider, and it just keeps getting wider the more The Mysteries are revealed to you. You need to feel that you deserve to be given access to The Mysteries of the Divine Feminine, challenging your previously held belief about your deservability to be directly accessing The Keepers of The Mysteries. Just shower yourself with love if you are challenged in any way. No other human being can honestly have control over your view of reality, because you are unique and your truth must be accessed and brought forward for you to evolve.

The Keepers of The Mysteries are the energy beings who know the secrets for immortality through the consciousness of the Divine Feminine and you must trust that these beings are real living energies who are allowing The Mysteries to be revealed to you now. Just create in you now a sacred space for this meditation to be introduced to The Keepers of The Mysteries now. Firstly make an offering and a commitment to utilizing The Mysteries in your life. Do this now. Do not ask to be shown anything sacred or secret without knowing you will create a space for this information in your life now. So just really go within and honestly examine your need for wanting the Sacred Mysteries to be revealed to you. Do not do this out of idle curiosity, but a genuine need to access the Sacred Mysteries.

You may like to go through the first meditation again, outlined in the beginning of the book, to reinforce your connection with The Keepers of The Mysteries of the Divine Feminine:

1) Anoint yourself

2) Allow yourself to receive

3) Breathe deeply, powerfully, rhythmically

4) Rock gently

5) Go to your heart center and feel you are entering a sacred space.

You may like to visualize yourself as part of a group I led in Peru with my guide, a Peruvian Sharmaness. There is a doorway on a barren mountain plain at Lake Titicaca called "Amarús Doorway". The Catholic Spaniards called it "The Devil's Doorway" and forbade anyone from having anything to do with it. Our guide invited my students and me to enter this rocky ledge and experience "immortality." Challenging yourself to experience "immortality" implies respect for yourself, and your "self"-respect will develop as you journey with The Keepers. The response from the students varied from, "I felt absolutely nothing," to feelings of extreme bliss and a heightened sense of awakening in their world. One student insisted that I had called her back before she experienced anything, I hadn't but the stories reveal that when the student is ready the teacher will appear. The most important thing to remember is surrendering your previously held belief about yourself.

To experience transcendence is indeed the most challenging thing a human can do. If you cannot respect yourself to experience transcendence you will remain stuck forever bound to return to Earth, re-hooking into the Karmic cycle again and again. This is dangerous for the soul because "it" knows it is basically repeating the same pattern and "it" feels lost and often abandoned. Treat your soul to some karmic clearing every day by intoning:

"I now give myself soul time."

"I now allow myself "self"-respect."

"Self-respect implies that I am free of guilt and harbor no resentment toward others."

"When I harbor a negative feeling toward others, I am loosing respect for myself, and I become disconnected from my immortal soul."

"I respect myself, therefore I respect all life."

The Secrets of The Divine Feminine can only be revealed to you in a space of self-respect. Self-respect becomes self love. You cannot have self love without self-respect.

All of humanity is on a quest for the realization of this "self" and the considerations in bringing forward this truth is going to be revealed as humanity awakens from its slumber and inertia. The ancient ones are patient and they wait. Time in the linear sense means nothing to them. So The Keepers just wait for those who seek the knowledge to awaken from the slumber of self-hatred. Humanity has many options now. Communications, technology allow for this awakening. This awakening will see no feeding on emotional expression through others, and it is important for those who choose to be bold to challenge themselves, and bring themselves into alignment with the magnificence that awaits them.

Freeing the soul from its slumber allows for the peace and oneness to be revealed from The Keepers of the Secrets of The Divine Feminine. This is a truth: The Keepers of The Mysteries are waiting, but they do not reveal themselves to you because you want instant gratification, or are a mere curiosity seeker.

You must not do this. You must not allow yourself this delusion because it is the biggest trap to realizing the "self." It is a false door that leads to extinction. Your truth will be extinguished, and your heart-centered, truth-filled world will just disconnect and observe and not partake in the creation when this happens. Just be humble and climb the ladder slowly one step at a time. Just close the door on fear and delusion and say goodbye to your old world.

Before you begin the following visualization exercise, it is important to give yourself space, free from your mind. Be aware of your breath; breathing in deeply, powerfully and rhythmically.

The Secret Garden Visualization

This visualization will help you feel this new transcendence.

Visualize yourself now as a child. Say to yourself right now: "I am a child." "This is my garden, it is pretty but I am bored in this garden, it's just silly for me being here. It's boring and silly, I am bored."

Suddenly a magical ladder appears, and you look at this ladder. Where does it lead? What do you do? Where does the ladder go? You cry; there is no answer; what do you do? You don't have an answer. Some "children" tell the ladder to go away, some foolishly climb blinded to where they are going. These children slip and crash, some die, some just sit and sulk and say it's too hard climbing ladders anyway. I'll just stay in this human garden and be pleasured and amuse myself with my toys and wait for mummy and daddy to look after me.

This is the space of delusion and fear. Because the child (you) doesn't know what you are here for or why "you" are having an incarnation anyway. You need reassurance in your human space, and you seek to find it outside yourself, in the arms of another person, in denial that you are the only one responsible for having the experience anyway. This is a time to recognize and reflect on why you have chosen to find yourself in the human garden.

This garden is like a garden of paradise. There are so many beautiful things on Earth. It is a treasure trove of beauty, yet we trash it, because we don't trust in the process of our own love and respect for ourselves not to trash it. When we trash it we trash a part of ourselves, and this part now needs to be brought back into balance. Balancing ourselves is essential now. To look at you and what you have created, requires a balanced perspective.

Find yourself now in your garden. Which part of the garden are you in? Wander around your garden now. Where do you find yourself? Who are you meeting? What is the state of the environment, the hedges, lawns and paths? Is there water in your garden? Look around at the nature; is there lots of vegetation? Is it over grown? Is it sunny, windy, raining, damp or cold? Engage the senses and really look hard. Is it day or night? What time of day is it, morning, afternoon or evening? Each question you ask yourself will code you to where you are at in your life right now.

Make a diary of your journey. Write a summary of where "you" are right now and begin the journey of self-discovery of The Divine Feminine Mysteries. Allow yourself to begin the ascent now.

You are safe and protected, provided you observe all around you and seek to find the answers to life's mysteries as you climb.

This is a time to acknowledge the climb. How fit are you for climbing? Both body and spirit have to be engaged to co-create. Live in the present. Just look at the ladder, your foot is on step one. What do I have to do to release, to climb the first step?

The first step is the hardest. The biggest pull of gravity against you will be all your attachments. Just look hard at your garden of attachments and unhook from them, just gently unhook from them, and say goodbye to them. This will be very painful. They will cry out for you and you have to be firm but gentle with all your attachments. This is your path and only "you" can ascend.

Breathe deeply, powerfully and rhythmically as you release. Just do it, knowing you cannot grow until you have let go of all attachments to earth you.

"I now let go of all attachments which ground me to illusion. I am now free to climb."

This is your adventure now. A journey begins with a feeling of adventure and freedom. You will feel the exhilaration of the new and untested. (The image of The Fool in The Tarot is an excellent example for the feeling of abandonment, yet excitement of leaving the old. The Fool is the first card in the deck.) You may like to reflect on the archetypes in The Tarot. The archetypes of the major Arcana in The Tarot are an excellent source for the climb to the world of The Mysteries, because they represent the totality of human experience. Working with a deck of Tarot cards will aid the imagery as you are connecting to the most powerful images of the human unconscious state. The karma of your life can be viewed in pictorial form and the images bringing to you in sharp focus the journey to your destination, which is immortality and accessing The Mysteries of the Divine Feminine. I have used Tarot cards every day privately and professionally since I was at university, and I am constantly astounded by the accuracy and power of the archetypical forces helping people understand and change lives. They are the blue print for the journey if you choose to work with these images to aid your journey. Just allowing yourself the pleasure of receiving the wisdom of The Tarot will provide focus for your adventure.

You can use The Tarot evoking The Keepers to provide you with the keys to unlocking your path to their wisdom.

The Mysteries of the Divine Feminine are now bringing to your life this sense of adventure. Begin the adventure of self discovery now by plotting your journey to a self-realized life. A self-realized life brings the mystery of creation to you in a magical and personal form. Allow The Mysteries to unfold gently on your journey. This is an adventure and has all the elements of the adventure. The adventure is the beginning of trust in the self to explore The Mysteries. Let the curtain open to reveal your act.

Before you begin the following visualization exercise, it is important to give yourself space, free from your mind. Be aware of your breath; breathing in deeply, powerfully and rhythmically.

Adventure of Self Discovery Visualization

Visualize yourself now on stage.

This is Act One.

You are free. Feel the freedom of being on stage now beginning your journey.

You are a performer. Witnessing your own performance now is an act of trust in yourself to create "you."

You are you and you need only "you" on stage. I am the fool. I am the adventurer.

My life begins as an adventure when I decided to reincarnate. My soul has the blue print and I put it in my backpack, when I incarnated.

The soul said,
"You have decided to find a lost part of yourself by being human. Your blue print for this journey is in the backpack.

Don't forget to really check it regularly because "you" can get "lost" down there being human. Just don't forget."

Remember the mission. Of course "you" are excited. There are so many adventures to be had, stories to be told, experiences to hold on to. You are excited, now you are at this space. Your adventure begins NOW.

Here you are on stage.

Now you are about to perform.

Let the performance begin!

To support your visualization journey:

Begin your breathing sequence, inviting The Keepers of The Mysteries in. They are here with you now as you enter your crypt or sacred cave. Acquaint yourself with your new environment. Feel it around you. You are in an unknown place within yourself and you need to familiarize yourself with this space.

You are curious, but this is a danger; curiosity at this point can get you into trouble.

Don't be just curious, this is self-sabotage.

Curiosity invites trouble.

Observe, be a witness to yourself and evoke protection. (I invite Anubis, the Egyptian deity and archetypal force, the jackal dog and guardian of perilous journeys to always protect me on these journeys.) Be aware.

Don't attempt to go into the unknown unless you are protected and you can trust and rely on protection. If you have never evoked protection or been familiar with it you need to stop and consider where you are going. Do this now.

"In the name of love and light and in the name of my absolute Divine Truth, I now ask for protection on my journey to meet The Keepers of The Mysteries of the Divine Feminine."

"I seek the wisdom to evolve my soul's path and live with peace and knowledge of what being human is and why I have incarnated to experience being human."

Imagine now you have a backpack with everything in your life in it. As you lay out the contents, they will reveal to you what you may be subconsciously holding onto.

The contents reveal three parcels.

Open them.

Let yourself experience these three separate aspects of yourself now.

These parcels represent what you have to release to journey further into your heart.

Bury them in the garden, or throw them into the ocean or release them to the sky.

Thank them and forgive them.

Bless them and dismiss them, and then walk away, back into the crypt/cave or space where you began your journey.

How do "you" feel? You may like to write down how you feel after this visualization.

The Keepers of The Mysteries of the Divine Feminine are sources of great and living power and they must be acknowledged as such. They are powerful eyes that watch you in the dark and seek to observe you and question why you want access to their world. They are loving, but they are also guarded. They must be respected as living powerful beings of Light. These souls are The Keepers of the Wisdom for the consciousness of The Divine Feminine and while not feared they demand respect. They are androgynous forms and do not have sexual functions as you in your human self see men and women. To The Keepers there is no division between the sexes and sexuality, as you know, it is not known to them as they have served incarnations in understanding these forms of expressing the soul's journey. Their eyes watch you in the dark. They are The Keepers of The Mysteries. The Mysteries are not for self gain or power over others and they seek to find within you, your understanding of this. These treasures bring you love, peace and all you need for a self-realized life, going beyond even "the self" to create the essence of the universal principle of order, peace and harmony. They bring bliss in the Divinely Feminine way. Softness, beauty, strength, power and above all "self"-respect and then after "self"-respect comes the merging with them in your human form. They can come to you when your merging of "self" is complete. This is the aim of your relationship with these beings of Light.

My earlier book, "Awaken your Immortal Intelligent Heart," (Glenane 2016) supports your understanding of "self" merging and for truly understanding the force of the heart's intelligence, in shaping your new relationship with these beings.

This relationship must be fostered through the relationship with the "self" which implies "self-respect" and your journey must embrace "self" at every opportunity. When the "self" is not acknowledged the "self" cannot function. *It is unable to function because the "self" creates barriers to its own awareness.* This is an important concept in understanding how the "self" plays itself out in the human drama of being human. The "self" always needs to respond to "itself" at every opportunity. To do this in your journey of being human is to acknowledge the "self" and introduce the "self" to the "self". Begin to form a relationship with your "self" now. To create this acknowledgment creates the joy in being human.

Ask yourself every day, *How did I acknowledge the "self" today?* To acknowledge the "self" is the beginning of "self-respect." I now know I must honor the "self" to create the space to grow awareness of myself as a being able to create a world within myself. The world within the "self" gives you access to the universal power to create any reality you want, for your absolute Divine Truth, which is a mergence with your Divinely Feminine form. Just acknowledging this truth implies that you are in a space of growth and acceptance of the "self" in its totality. Your view of yourself is created through the love and power you give yourself, which in turn magnetizes others to you for your growth.

Now that you are beginning to feel this "self" growing in you, you need to feed this "self" with love and to have others admire it. A baby is admired, commented on and petted because adults and other children "see" something in the baby that is pure. They see baby's purity of "self." There is a "self" here although the baby's consciousness doesn't even know it. To regain this service of "self" is to feed it with love and admiration daily. The "self" has to be born again like the Immortal Scarab (the Ancient Egyptian symbol of rebirth). We too have to feel and acknowledge this new "self." Look at the baby again. She has no consciousness of the day before, inappropriate behaviors, hurts and betrayals. All "she" experiences is the purity of the new day and an acknowledgment of what this day's potential can bring her.

To allow this "self" to be born, you may like to find a still space within and without for the following visualization:

Before you begin the following visualization exercise, it is important to give yourself space, free from your mind. Be aware of your breath; breathing in deeply, powerfully and rhythmically.

The Scarab Visualization

Begin this visualization now as "you" allow your new "self" to be born again.

Breathe deeply three times and infuse the body's cells with newness.

Evoke the consciousness of the Scarab and ask it to fill every cell with the memory of only "the now."

"I now command my cellular memory to accept 'new' frequencies."

"I am now reborn for this day and every day thereafter."

The Miracle of Mysteries Revealed through the Hearts Secrets

"Today is the beginning of my new life to 'self.'"

"Today is the beginning of trust for me 'now.'"

Your beginning of "your" new day creates liberation of just acceptance of what this day will bring. Just try for one day to have absolutely no agenda for it at all. Evoke the Scarab. Now just feel the essence of the Scarab in you as you create with the elements, for your new day today:

"I am just surrendering all expectations of anyone or thing."

This shift creates in you the need to find in yourself your absolute truth for that day. Your absolute truth for that day creates a oneness and uniqueness for all of creation. Try now. I am now creating this day for my soul. This is my soul day. This is the day my soul needs, all it needs. I surrender to the energy essence and life force of the Scarab to create in my newness. My newness now creates growth in my soul and your immortal soul is fed with this nourishment now. This nourishment for all of divinity is your soul food and the essence of your divinity is now creating in you oneness with all of creation. Write down this day in your diary. Journal the events and look at how the patterns emerge. The joy will be the soul talking to you. This is my soul's day. This is my soul's journey. This is my opportunity to allow myself the absolute divinity within myself.

The journey to trust in The Mysteries creates a special relationship with all the forces assisting in creation. These forces will become apparent to you in your journey. You need to recognize the forces of creation as having special significance for you now as you take yourself inward on your quest for self hood. The quest for self hood is the most important requirement in being human and must not be ignored. Now is a time to recognize and hold true to your core identity. There must be in your life strength to cope and a core identity, which supports change, which comes with increasing frequency. Your core identity comes through "self nurturing" and "self-respect." Our belly center is our core. My books to support the developing of your core identity are; "The Alchemies of Isis Embodiment through The High Priestess" and "Embodying the Divine Masculine of All Truth through The High Priest." (Glenane 2016)

"The Keepers will give you a "signature" for their presence. It is usually through "sound." Allow yourself to be embraced by "sound." If you can, try and remember the sound and re-create it if possible. Whatever space you feel yourself entering, must be felt and observed within you, as you follow the path to uncover The Mysteries of the Divine Feminine. You need to feel that The Mysteries are revealing themselves to you, as you open your awareness lens wide. Consciousness is endless. What do "you" do with all this consciousness? You need to feel that this consciousness can be funneled into your reality. You need to be very specific here. You are actually aiming for a target in universal consciousness. The target for universal consciousness is love. You must feel this message.

Before you begin the following visualization exercise, it is important to give yourself space, free from your mind. Be aware of your breath; breathing in deeply, powerfully and rhythmically.

Visualization for Accessing Sound

This brief visualization will assist you in accessing the sound of The Keepers.

Imagine yourself now dialing the number to get a person. Now listen to the sound. There must be a space of nothingness and receptivity before you hear anything. Just feel this now, and allow yourself this empty space.

Allow yourself to listen. As humans we must learn to be in the pregnant listening space, before being given the secrets. The secrets belong to the listener. The listener hears but truth is hard to find and mostly not listened to when heard anyway.

To make sure you "hear" your truth, write down in your journal your reflections:

How did The Keepers present themselves?

What is their signature for you?

What did I do to get to this space?

What did they say to me?

The Keepers are always available to show and share because of their custodial nature, however there is also reluctance too. There is a protective and watchful aspect to The Keepers, so you must attune to their vibration. This is very important in keeping the attention of The Keepers.

While in Cairo after a teaching tour I was able to observe while on my personal pilgrimage on the Giza Plateau how a Keeper of the Secrets of a Tomb of a vizier was actually evaluating my ability to respond to what was really in this ancient crypt.

After the usual man/woman preliminaries were out of the way, he announced his position in this tomb, i.e. I'm not a guard but an employee of the Department of Antiquities. Two hours later I emerged from this tomb with an understanding and depth of appreciation not only for the employee (custodian), The Keeper's love of all this vault contained, but the pleasure of seeing some very extraordinary and powerful glimpses into the real nature of this vault's energy.

Respect for The Keeper, acknowledgment of The Keeper, and love of what The Keeper is looking after is always needed before any real understanding can take place.

Try this exercise in a shop or place which houses beautiful things, artifacts, jewelry, paintings, etc. and don't waste the time of The Keeper, the store attendant or owner by being a curiosity seeker. You get no respect and no information.

On my teaching tour to these countries, my own initiation with The Keepers had begun six months earlier on Love Island on Lake Titicaca in Peru. I felt the raw power of Pacha Mama (the Peruvian name for Mother Earth). Vomiting and weak, I led my students to the small amphitheater on top of a mountain; she appeared saying she demanded my personal Calvary for "her" to be born in me. This is her story.

Before you begin the following visualization exercise, it is important to give yourself space, free from your mind. Be aware of your breath; breathing in deeply, powerfully and rhythmically.

Pacha Mama's Story

"The journey home creates in you now your belief that you are solely responsible for everything that happens to you. You have opened up the new doorway to a new level of consciousness in accessing The Mysteries of the Divine Feminine. The access to a new level of consciousness has been activated and this is indeed a powerful statement of truth in your reality. You are showing the world by your philosophy to receiving The Mysteries that you can be in a space of forgiveness for yourself for being asleep for so long. Why? You may ask yourself, have I not been allowed to partake in the miracle of my own creation? Why have these 'secrets' not been able to be accessed by me before this time?"

"There is a period of despair, when you realize that 'you' have been asleep for so long and 'you' are angry that 'you' are left in the dark. The most exciting and terrifying part of your journey comes at the moment of awakening, when 'you' really 'wake' up to your limitless possibilities in being human. The Mysteries of the Divine Feminine are creating this new consciousness in you now and you are able to feel the energy love and drive this newness creates. Trying to create a new view of your humanness is now a challenge in your life. Your life is now embracing the challenge of knowing you are awake enough to enact The Mysteries and The Keepers of The Mysteries are living powerful entities, focused on your ascent into a New View of Being Human."

This emerging awareness will leave a most powerful impression on your consciousness as you struggle to really embrace your new view of being human. The Keepers of The Mysteries of the Divine Feminine are awaiting such an awakening and you're "groping in the dark" to find the light allows them to find you. You are "groping in the dark" when you do not trust that the wise ones in the shadows are watching you. Stop, and stop "groping" now. Affirm that you request The Mysteries be available to you and that you receive the welcoming love of The Keepers. Just stop now. You have been "groping" at all levels. Humans grope in the dark when they "feel in the dark" about something.

You need to stop and ask The Keepers of The Mysteries to help you forward the answer. Feel their warmth, attention and gentle whispering. They will not crowd you, but if you are still you will find them. They cannot be accessed without this stillness from you, and acknowledgment of "you" to them.

Your earlier journal entries will support your respect for The Keepers' wisdom, by stopping your mind and feeling the stillness. Feel the darkness. Feel the darkness now.

Allow yourself to merge in this space and really go into it. When you do this, you are feeling the Feminine in you.

You are empty, receptive, nurturing yourself.

It is from this space, that you can journey to meet The Keepers of The Mysteries. Let them whisper to you now.

Note now in your journal their response to your "dark" question.

I am "In the dark;" I want the Keepers to give me the answer.

The surrender in the dark is the next step in accessing The Keepers of The Mysteries of the Divine Feminine. You must be prepared to fully surrender in the dark, and trust those watchful eyes to assist you. You need to feel empty, and this emptiness creates a void; a nothingness similar to the sense of a pregnant woman, feeling, waiting for her baby to be born. Try and create this in your consciousness now. Just create a space of being in the dark; an emptiness and surrender.

Before you begin the following visualization exercise, it is important to give yourself space, free from your mind. Be aware of your breath; breathing in deeply, powerfully and rhythmically.

Surrender Visualization

Visualize yourself in the dark now. Just feel the emptiness. Really feel this space. Just go into yourself and feel this. Do this now, while creating a meditative space and protection around you. The feeling of absolute emptiness must surround you now.

I feel empty.

I feel sad, I feel alone.

Now I need to surrender to bring in my Keepers.

Bringing in The Keepers of The Mysteries requires that you need to honor the surrender and be receptive to the surrendering process. There is no harder task than surrendering what you have loved. For example, a death of a loved one and what that person meant to you. The surrender acknowledges that you must give up the struggle, the fight with the ego and subconscious.

Finally SURRENDER is the most important acknowledgment of your humanness and your fragility. I am fragile; I can't keep holding on to this; I just can't understand it.

Why? You ask yourself, as you struggle for an answer to your humanness. This humanness is the very struggle. The struggle is in the humanness.

"I now surrender my humanness and seek the wisdom of The Keepers of The Mysteries of the Divine Feminine to be with me now."

Now list your human struggles.

Write them down.

I need to find an answer for my humanness in this situation.

The Miracle of Mysteries Revealed through the Hearts Secrets

I now surrender all expectations of myself in this quest to find an answer at the soul's level.

Assembling the Jig Saw of Being Human

What creates in you right now the desire to know The Mysteries?

Why are The Mysteries of the Divine Feminine so important anyway and why are The Keepers needed?

The Mysteries are the creation of all that is whole and balanced. A whole and balanced person; a whole and balanced universe are what The Mysteries represent.

You as the Seeker of The Mysteries of the Divine Feminine must want this balance within yourself first, and in this wanting, you create in this balance, a great love of all humanity.

All of humanity is a quest for this balance now. Create the quest for the balance within you now by allowing yourself the growth to really be part of "The One."

"The One" is the sum total of all existence and The Mysteries are "This One."

I am "One" so I am. I am "One." I am "One": "The Oneness" is me now. I am "One," and "The Oneness" is all around me now. I am "One."

All of life is a challenge to experience oneness.

The Mysteries create this "Oneness" now.

Believe in your ability to create "Oneness" now.

Your life is a cycle to create "Oneness" and as you crawl around into the spiral going within and within, you begin to experience the hypnotic effect of the hole and your vision becomes diffused and it is in this space that The Mysteries become revealed to you.

Before you begin the following visualization exercise, it is important to give yourself space, free from your mind. Be aware of your breath; breathing in deeply, powerfully and rhythmically.

Visualization for Assembling the Jig Saw of Being Human

Stare for one whole minute, traveling inward on the spiral breathing deeply, slowly and rhythmically. Crawl into The Mystery and become one with it. It's a mystery to me. No it's not. You don't have to be mystified ever again. There is no mystery and what's more just surrender your concept of what The Mysteries could be anyway.

The brilliance of being human is in the knowledge that this spiral can take you anywhere you like. For example:

Visualize yourself now, and just get into the spiral, just go into the spiral and allow yourself to journey in the spiral.

Just journey within and allow "you" the experience of knowing that "you" are connected to The Mysteries, as you journey within.

This is a time of just recognizing the spiral and journey within to yourself.

You need to feel the completeness in doing this, and you need to feel the peace as well as you go into your third eye to explore what The Mysteries bring to your life now.

Experience the joy of The Mysteries and bring to your life the peace of The Mysteries.

Just feel the completeness of The Mysteries now as you create your "you" and just feel the energy, life force and magic coming to you in The Mysteries.

All of life is a quest for The Mysteries to be revealed to you, and you need to feel the joy and love of The Mysteries being part of "you" now.

Just feel the nothingness, and emptiness of your inward cycle.

Just visualize yourself circling inward, inward and inward until you feel ready to stop.

It is at this point that the other you is ready to be revealed to. Just feel the energy of The Mysteries now.

You need to feel the joy and love of The Mysteries now. They are living energies and living truths. Just continue to feel them now. This is a time to reveal and feel the joy of The Mysteries now.

The goddess is in the spiral, and you need to spiral inward.

Just spiral inward, keep spiraling inward.

Be the "one" and allow yourself to become the "one." I am the "one," and I create in the "one."

"The one" is in me now, as I gather me and go within to "my creation."

Just believe in "your" creation now. This is a time to go within and connect to this "creation" now.

The Mysteries reveal themselves to you in many surprising ways when you attune to The Keepers of The Mysteries of the Divine Feminine. The Mysteries are all around you and your attunement to The Mysteries only serves to bring you closer to The Keepers. See The Keepers, always ready to show you The Mystery, when "you" are in a space of "suspension." This state of "suspension" can be seen to be a state of absolute surrender to the power of the goddess who is the Mystery Keeper. There will be one specific Mystery for you as you unfold your petals and begin to feel the magic of creation. To begin to explore The Mysteries is being very sensitive to all around you and allowing the space of "suspension" to enfold you.

"I now allow this space of 'suspension' to enfold me, and I am embraced by the feeling of 'suspension.'"

I create so I am. I am leaving behind the local energies, which distract me, and create a state of "suspension" in me right now. You need to feel the power of the truth of the "suspension," which brings The Keepers in.

1) *You need to find the focus within first and know you are forwarding the focus.*

2) *You are now feeling the "suspension," and allowing The Keepers of The Mysteries to be made available to you. There will be one assigned to you at the beginning of your journey. Just bring The Keepers to you now. You are now creating space to really find the peace and happiness The Keepers of The Mysteries bring.*

Allowing yourself to feel embraced by the energies, helps you transcend the limitations of your humanness. You need to feel this suspension and be with it.

Before you begin the following visualization exercise, it is important to give yourself space, free from your mind. Be aware of your breath; breathing in deeply, powerfully and rhythmically.

The Spider – "Aracne's" Visualization

Imagine now you are focused.

I am focused.

Feel yourself as a spider creating her web.

"Why am I creating this web?"

This web catches flies. I only want flies, no other insect. A large insect will break my web and humans will destroy my web. I need to focus to catch my food, and "make" the focus your intention.

Imagine you are watching the spider with focused concentration.

Take a leap.

You have to get to that particular part of the wall or ledge.
This is suspension.

You will get there or not.

You are suspended until your rope/web is anchored to a secure space.

Do not create your web in a space of flexibility.

You must be in a space of quietness to create your Mystery.

You begin to feel the timelessness in the suspension and the sacred alchemy of timelessness is the space of The Keepers of The Mysteries of Divine Feminine. This is the space of alchemy, the beginning of helplessness in the Mystery of suspension, of nothingness this is the space that must be created for The Mysteries to be revealed.

This is the space of the great void where The Keepers hold the secrets. All of life is in the state of suspension. The web of creation cannot be without this suspension. In this space there is nothing and everything and all of life begins again. All of life is in this space and you must feel the power and journey within all of life lying in this space. (Refer to my book "Awaken your Immortal Intelligent Heart" – The Black Heart) (Glenane 2016)

Before you begin the following visualization exercise, it is important to give yourself space, free from your mind. Be aware of your breath; breathing in deeply, powerfully and rhythmically.

The following visualization will help you develop this feeling of suspension and freedom:

Focus on an objective. Create the space for it to take place.

Visualize yourself in the space of suspension, where all else is obsolete except this moment.

Nothing is important except this moment.

The Keepers become activated now.

Call them; find your ledge and then jump.

You have uncovered the Mystery of being human.

This is an important time.

"I now honor and love my 'she' enough to grow 'her' and to birth her into a new life."

This is important. All life comes from the principle of "The She" and all life is from "The She." "The She" is "She." I am from the principle of "The She." The Goddess of All Light is part of the "The She" and any light energy from your unconscious can be this "She" as Sekhmet was for Robert Masters, author of "The Goddess Sekhmet" (Masters 2010) or Isis was for Cleopatra.

The struggle with "The She" is the struggle in your identity to suffering. You feel as a sensitive giving human being that you must struggle with the vibration of suffering. This struggle is in acknowledging your beginning respect of yourself. You must recognize when you just don't have to struggle in suffering and when enough is enough.

The Keepers are that, "Keepers." You are The Keepers so you must have something worthwhile to "keep" as you "keep" the secrets hidden away aware of who approaches. You are allowing yourself to observe all who want the wisdom to buy them peace and love. What is it you observe in us, your seekers? What do you see in us, and how do you find us, when lost, alienated, miserable search for answers you just can't fathom.

The Keepers are observing you now, and they are listening to you. They are listening and they are waiting for your reasons to want admittance to the secrets. The Keepers are respecters of all and they respect you and your truth to feel the power and strength you need to explore The Mysteries. They will not test you, but they will expect that you are sincere and honest in your search for The Mysteries.

The Keepers hold the key. The key is the truth and you need to forward this truth in you now.

The details of your search they already know, but they are looking for the intelligence of your answer.

Your answers to your questions must be answered by "you" first.

This is the way. Answer your questions to you first.

Try and answer your own questions first.

Just answer your own questions first, and then they can assist you.

Allow yourself to hear your own answers first.

When you try and answer your own question, before you "parrot" for an answer from The Keepers, you are respecting your own spirituality, and questioning your own ability to really work with the answer you seek.

This is such a challenge, because you need to have the formula partially formed in your consciousness. The Keepers need to see this study, this application as you approach them. This is needed by the aspiring seeker.

The seeker "seeks." The Keepers, "keep."

Seek = Keep.

I speak, The Keepers Keep.

I give a bit, you give a bit.

The human consciousness can only take so much in its enfoldment as the codings have been broken, damaged and the need to get these codings in alignment first must be done. The seeker has to recognize that the codings are damaged, broken and like a jigsaw puzzle, must fit them all together. This is very important. You may have broken codings around poverty, over lifetimes and these are repairs, which must be made by The Keepers of The Mysteries. You can ask The Keepers to repair restructure and re-code these codings, like making a rope strong before you climb any higher up the mountain.

If you are experiencing difficulties in seeking your answers for peace, you may like to say this affirmation:

"In the name of Love and Light and my absolute Divine Truth may I have these codings repaired and restructured now."

The Keepers are attuning you now as you embrace this new way of connecting to your humanness. This humanness brings with it all that it can for your life as you embark on your new adventure in being human. There is an adventure in being human and you are embracing this now. The Keepers of The Mysteries will gently guide and lead you to embrace The Mysteries of the Divine Feminine. You need to feel that your codings are being reconnected because the Keepers cannot work with all your broken codings and faulty wirings, through lifetimes of abuse. The abuse was sustained through many incarnations in being human. To restructure these codings will be done now as you create a new reality of living. The new reality of living is one of absolute trust and surrender in all of life to give you your power and direction. This is a time to create this new direction in your living now and allow yourself to create a new way of living for yourself.

"I now ask The Keepers of The Mysteries of the Divine Feminine to completely repair, re-align, recode and re-adjust my Mt DNA to be fully able to bring through The Mysteries of the Divine Feminine consciousness. I ask that this be taking place now."

Please consider the Mt DNA activation from my book, "Awaken your Immortal Intelligent Heart," (Glenane 2016) as a primary source for recoding DNA.

The Keepers keep. This is it. They keep. The secrets are kept. Revealing a secret is a shared sacred trust and The Keepers are revealing the secrets to you the seeker, because "you" have created conditions in your consciousness to create these amazing secrets to be reactivated in you now. Just revealing the secrets to yourself first is a gift of knowing that you are worthy to have absolute peace and bliss in being human. Being human is not about suffering and despair. It is about transcending the limitations of humanness, and knowing you are allowed to think like this. I allow myself to transcend the limitations of my humanness and go beyond these limitations. This is my birthright. Yes it is my birthright not to suffer and to be traumatized. You just say to yourself,

"I am now in a time and place in my heart's intelligence, where I do not allow myself to be limited by my humanness."

The Keepers are watching and they assist you, when they know you really want to experience your humanness, which goes beyond the cruelties and betrayals placed upon you over lifetimes.

In initiations in ancient civilizations the initiates were required to undergo rigorous purifications, beginning from a young age. Not so now. All you need is an open heart to change your life from what it is and free your mortality to immortality. You are allowed to think like this. All of humanity is being initiated now.

Accept this initiation within yourself now.

The process of the discovery of your new self starts with your cells. These are the magnifiers and amplifiers of The Keepers' wisdom. The Keepers will now bring new information to your cellular memory by restructuring and re-coding, and re-aligning your cellular memory. Your cellular memory can be traced to your immortal self. Your cellular memory is the storehouse of your incarnations of belief in your truth. Your cellular memory is the beginning of change for you now so you must feel the vibration of your cellular memory awaken in you your endless possibility in your humanness. To believe that your cellular memory is able to be re-coded is an act of trust in yourself as a being who can have all the knowledge downloaded to you at any instant. The storehouse of knowledge can be opened up and you are able to find in your life all you need to create all you want to know about the secrets of the Divine Feminine. You need now to re-code your cellular memory to rid itself of any fears and limitations about this happening.

You may like to affirm:

"I am fully open and receptive to the belief that the cellular memory is capable of strong new frequencies for my humanness. This is now part of my genetic make-up. I now know I am capable of these re-codings, my consciousness can take this now."

Always The Keepers are aware of the challenges in being human and they know human kind is collectively striving for discovering the secrets. Actually the secrets are encoded in your own genetic blue print but they need to be sought and activated again and again. Keep knowing and trusting yourself to know what you are asking for. I know I need the secrets to bring to my life; love, freedom, wisdom and truth. These are the secrets of being human and you now need to feel that the Mystery of the Sphinx is now open to you, too. The Mystery of the Sphinx contains the blue print for being human and the strong body of the Sphinx has survived time itself. Our bones carry the blue print (our genetic material), and past karma is encoded in the bones of our own body. You can look at an anatomy map of your own body. Look at a skeleton, and imagine this skeleton is your own body's message to you. You need to gaze in visualization on your own skeleton, and go into the cellular memory of your bones. Trace the history of your bones, track any bone breakages and look at your teeth as well, any root canal fillings and damage, etc.

Your spinal structure is the foundation of your karmic and earthly existence. Your spine will reveal the essence of who you are and why you are here anyway. Your spine corresponds in its codings to your ancestry at soul and biological level. Making a study of your own spine will reveal to you much about your personal ability to really understand the nature of your illnesses or disease, which are fears out of control. The spine is an electrical transmitter for all information you need for your journey of truth, love, wisdom and freedom.

All a human wants is encoded in these words:

- *Truth corresponding to the element of Earth = When we are truth-filled we are earthed*
- *Love corresponding to the element of Water = When we are self loving we are flowing like water*
- *Wisdom corresponding to the element of Fire = When we are wise our passion burns brightly*
- *Freedom corresponding to the element of Air = When we are free we float on air*

The Sphinx, the most ancient and sensitive monument on the planet has a spine because the body on the Pharaoh (or Jackal-headed Anubis, refer to Robert Temple "The Sphinx Mystery") (Temple 2009) is a representative of the nature of human's struggle to attain immortality and knowledge of the Divine Feminine Mysteries. So what you are searching for is within yourself anyway, and your spine reflects your struggle.

The search is actually encoded in you and your search must begin with the "self." The "self" has the key to the wisdom of creation, because the "self" is the creation. Every cell in your body has the genetic code for all of life both earthly and celestial.

What we, "The Keepers," do is allow you the keys to the riddle. We provide answers to help you find the keys. We provide answers to help you find the riddle for being on Earth, so when you discover us, you are acknowledging you are aware enough to want answers for why truth in love eludes you. You ask yourself in your dreams why the joy of being in love with yourself is such a struggle and why you seek this outside yourself with another human being who is lost anyway. How crazy to seek in someone else what you can't find within yourself. Don't try, just don't do this, and don't seek to look for in another human being man or woman what you are searching for in yourself. What you are searching for within yourself is your ability to find your power. All humans want is to find their own power. Finding your own power is your weapon in your human existence and the secrets in the paws of The Sphinx are in your paws, your Sphinx – "Yourself!"

Believing in your own ability to solve the riddle of your humanness is the answer you must seek to find within yourself now. You are able to do this in so many ways, in being able to feel the power of who you are. Feeling the power of who you are helps you answer the "Riddle of The Sphinx" inside you. To feel the power of who you are is not to feel a victim of any circumstance in your life at all. This is a time to recognize that you are able to really trust in the forces, which magnetize themselves to you when you seek the answers to your own divinity and power.

Before you begin the following visualization exercise, it is important to give yourself space, free from your mind. Be aware of your breath; breathing in deeply, powerfully and rhythmically.

Visualization – The Sphinx

Draw "The Sphinx" over you now energetically through a visualization and feel the energy and protection of the Pharaoh – Lion or Jackal-headed Anubis. Really ask The Keepers to bring the Riddle of The Sphinx to yourself because The Sphinx is you anyway and this is the biggest riddle of all because you hold the answer to why you have a disease. What is your disease called? This disease can also include addictions, i.e. gambling, shopping, depression, anxiety disorder, etc. This disease is your messenger. The message must be listened to very carefully as you seek to understand your riddle.

In visualization ask now to feel The Keepers magnetize themselves toward you as you journey into your truth. You need to feel The Keepers really magnetize themselves to you so you can feel the holy joy and oneness of them now.

You need to acknowledge to yourself that you are ready to have The Keepers' magnetic presence all around you like winged ones. Feel their powerful eyes and feel their essence and oneness envelop you as you discover your ancestry. Your ancestry at soul level is being made available now. Allow yourself the holy and trusted presence of yourself now. You are a Divine being; one with all The Keepers. Have absolutely no fear as you surrender to these beings. All of life is an expression and experience of

The Miracle of Mysteries Revealed through the Hearts Secrets

yourself as you bring to your life your Divine truth about your being. Your "being" is "being." It is essence made manifest, and made into oneness. Feel this now, as you embark on your power trip. Now just acknowledge that your life now opens "you" up to your own power to discover yourself now through The Keepers of The Mysteries of the Divine Feminine.

The message from The Keepers of The Mysteries is very simple. To trust in them is going to be your truth, and your challenge. Your truth and your challenge are to trust them and to allow them into your life. You are truth made manifest with them, and you are very aware now of their sacred presence all around you if you have journeyed so far into yourself so far in reading this transmission. Your challenge now, that you are aware of their presence, is to live their truth in your life, and allow yourself your belief in your own ability to think outside the square and become multidimensional in your thinking.

You have a "problem." Every day there is a "problem." Every hour there is a "problem"; your culture and belief patterns create problems in you. One way of acknowledging old karmas coming to the surface is to say to yourself:

"When I have a problem, I am dealing with old karmas and cultural belief patterns."

Good: This is a board game.

You know where you are starting from, i.e. I have a problem with my tax bill, I have a problem with my disobedient child, I have a problem with my lover who is not faithful to me. The list is endless.

Try now, listing your current problems. List them one by one, and see now clearly how you are dealing with them. How am I dealing with this problem?

1) *What karma is involved? Poverty consciousness, relationship/ abandonment/ betrayal, disease/emotional/physical/spiritual, self worth?*

2) *What are my (or society's) belief patterns around this problem?*

3) *What are my personal subconscious fears around this issue or problem?*

By listing all the <u>obstacles</u>, one by one, you are unraveling all the patterns of belief around your fear or problem. Good, you know what you are dealing with.

This list is demonstrating how your past pattern has dealt with the problem.

Now, you say, I will look at all those negatives; list them, one by one. Wow, what a way of dealing with a problem, piling on all those negatives. This is not a good start to solving your problem. Wrap up all the obstacles now, (do it physically, like wrapping a parcel) and go to The Keepers, and hand all the problem/obstacles to The Keepers now. They will take it now, and show you a new way of looking at solving your life problems.

The riddle of being human is the riddle of creation itself. The riddle of yourself is to observe yourself as you play out your own games you have constructed in your awareness of yourself. You need to feel the energy, life force and magic of oneness with yourself as you begin the spiral dance of creation. If the riddle of being human is the riddle of creation itself, "why" you ask, are you so confused all the time? "Why is there no linear straight line to being human?" It appears like a jungle and you have to watch for unseen enemies all the time.

Your enemies are always your fears as you struggle against unseen forces everywhere. You now need to feel the connection with the great mother, who creates all. She is one with you now as you journey inward on your spiral dance. Your life now is one of creation with the unseen forces of creation. All of life is a test of invisible forces to leave you fearful and broken or healed and rejuvenated. All struggles, enemies and fears are really friends. You need now to witness any struggle and just allow it to be your friend, not your enemy. The very second you see yourself as having opposition, you create fear in you, and you set up barriers which stop you from creating with the forces that have created the barrier anyway. In other words, you can create with the forces you "see" as being destructive. They are only forces; your fear gives them power against you.

Before you begin the following visualization exercise, it is important to give yourself space, free from your mind. Be aware of your breath; breathing in deeply, powerfully and rhythmically.

The Breath of Creation Visualization

Breathe The Keepers into you now as you embrace the breath of creation. Breath is creation made manifest and your creation is through creation itself, the creative aspects of yourself is breath.

Breath is the most creative act you can carry out as you bring the goodness of life to yourself now.

Practice the breath and The Keepers know you are there.

Your breath alerts The Keepers to your presence and your breath alerts you to your own power with us.

The breath brings stillness and the breath brings power.

You acknowledge yourself with the breath every time you open up to the wonder of yourself. Your breath just creates a cellular change in you and you become the matrix of yourself. Your cellular change is now upon you as you bring breath to your cells.

Visualize yourself going into your own cells and coding them for change in consciousness. Your cellular memory just feeds itself as you bring to your life all that you want for your life now. The cells are the messengers and the cells carry memory. Breath changes the matrix of the cells so they can carry the new information. Allow the new information now to be encoded in you now, as you open your breath to the cells, changing the cells' construction and bringing "The Keepers of The Mysteries" into your cells. We are in your cells when you breathe us in.

The energy you bring to this new aspect of yourself will bring to your life a sense of wonder and you will experience your absolute joy in being human. This is a human's birthright. All humans have the right to all information about The Mysteries. But The Mysteries themselves are those very things that keep humans "in the dark" because they do not want to work for the information they so desperately want.

You must be aware of your society's restriction on you having the blue print to the consciousness of the Divine Feminine, and also be aware of the fear in loving yourself by not allowing yourself space to journey into yourself. This is the most troubling aspect of your life and you need to recognize that you deserve to bring to your life your own blue print for being human and why you have incarnated anyway. You must bring to your life all that "you" need for your journey of trust in allowing the process to take place in the first place.

You must feel that you are in a space of receiving and that this is receiving. The receiving of the wisdom from The Keepers is a very big responsibility to yourself, because it will change the way you relate to your world and you will feel the energy, freedom and passion for all of creation.

Being alive to the special presence of all around you is going to open The Mysteries to you. You must be aware of every moment being synchronized. It is an invisible world, but we are not invisible at all, we are very visible to your third eye and to your intuition. Every day just count up the coincidences and list them. Be alive and aware of the speeding up of your life when you become aware of this web. Life is a web and the web just keeps vibrating; you put out a thought and the thought reverberates throughout the universe.

Try putting out thoughts and watch them boomerang back to you. You must be aware of the subtle delicacy of thought. When thoughts are positive, the lines are strong; the web lines are straight and go straight out to the target. This creates more energy for more webs that go out that are straight and strong. Negative thoughts toward others create tangled webs, painful sticky webs full of fear. See these lines as sticky and tangled.

All of life is a journey to realize your absolute truth and you need to keep your webs straight and strong. Positive thought creates increased synchronicity. Fear only closes down the circulatory. Webs become sticky, tangled and weak and there becomes no structuring your life. You are lost and we The Keepers can't communicate with you.

The truth of The Keepers of The Mysteries are now enabling you to access so much more in your life. The Keepers' truth is one with all of life. All of life is the life The Keepers hold. The Keepers hold The Mysteries. For you to access them, and live them, brings freedom and bliss in being human. You need to feel this in you now as you create your absolute trust in what The Mysteries will give you. You create much power and it is electrical and radiates all around you. You will feel extraordinary life force and absolute Divine essence of oneness with all.

A love of The Mysteries is a true gift. To love The Mysteries themselves just drives you to the brink of yourself. You just need to feel now the love of The Mysteries themselves. They are a living form. They are truth, and they are light. To love The Mysteries is a gift of creation and oneness. I create in oneness with The Mysteries, and I am one with The Mysteries. I create in oneness with The Mysteries now and The Mysteries are one with me. Really allow your love of The Mysteries creates in you now your belief in your truth through all of creation. All of creation is with the principle of trust and sharing; trust and share in The Mysteries now. Trust and share in your truth now. You need to allow yourself now to see The Mysteries as tangible, living energies. Just trust and share in your truth now. The Mysteries themselves are here.

Just feel The Mysteries as intelligences in your heart now.

The Keepers of The Mysteries of the Divine Feminine are living embodiments of Divine Feminine energy. The Divine Feminine is the ultimate quest in the supremacy of the Feminine function as a creative and order-creating force in the universe. The universe has many diverse aspects. The Feminine is one aspect, and the Divine Feminine is this creativity made manifest. Your definition of yourself will change when you are in our vibration. It is one of absolute beauty in the essence of self, which is BLISS. The Bliss-filled "self" radiates joy.

Before you begin the following visualization exercise, it is important to give yourself space, free from your mind. Be aware of your breath; breathing in deeply, powerfully and rhythmically.

Bliss Visualization

See a bliss-filled energy, radiating joy similar to a bubble.

See a bubble now.

As you do, breathe in deeply three times:

Visualize a bubble. It is luminous, rainbow infused and very beautiful. It just glows; a bliss-filled individual just glows all the time from the inside. Now bring that bubble to yourself and just feel the luminous rainbow-filled bubble just getting bigger, more luminous; strong and luminous.

Really find the luminosity of The Keepers, now this is the essence of your divinity in human form.

Please visualize yourself in this way now.

You are bliss-filled now as you embrace this luminous self now.

The Divine Feminine self is bliss-filled and loves. Love her now.

The Keepers bring to you a sense of respect for yourself. They are really unafraid to allow you to really go into the heart of yourself and respect yourself. So you need to feel their awesome energy, which brings to you now self-respect. Your self-respect grows when you are one with The Keepers. They feel this self-respect and they encourage and validate your sense of "self"-respect. This is a time to validate that sense of self-respect in every cell of your body. Don't respect a living thing until you respect yourself and bring to yourself your Mystery. The sense of mystery is in self-respect, which comes before self-love. The respect of self is what we are teaching you now. Just feel the freedom, which comes with self-respect.

I respect myself enough to have around me people who respect themselves as well. I have in my life the truth behind all living things. I am one with the self-respecting ones. I am one with the great ones. The Keepers say there is no fear when I respect myself. I am respecting myself now, and I am journeying into make my life one of self-respect now.

The oneness that comes with self-respect brings to you now your belief that The Mysteries are real living energies. The Mysteries are in fact everywhere. Every-time we gaze in wonder at a sunset, a baby being born, the miracle of just observing nature, we are partaking in The Mysteries and the sacredness of The Mysteries cannot be categorized in a way which limits them in a form in anyway. They are formless and of the void. They come from a space beyond mind, beyond thinking and rationalization. They are from the deep heart of the Mother herself and they are one with her in every way.

The deep heart of the Mother of creation is endless. It is endless love, endless life and endless oneness. The oneness of all is the endless oneness of everything. Your observance of yourself just keeps growing inside you and you feel the endless pull of creation. You are one with the endless pull of creation in your endless search for your lost parts. Your lost parts are scattered everywhere and you have to observe them and retrieve them. Honor yourself by admitting to yourself that your lost scattered bits need retrieving. You need to feel that these lost scattered bits bring hope to you for your journey now. You are one with the journey into clearing your own karma. The Keepers teach you to find within yourself your relationship with your lost karma.

Finding your relationship with your lost karma just allows you to focus on your own truth. Your lost soul bits are scattered all over your universe and your job in human form is to find them, like a dog finds a bone. Observe how the dog hunts for the bone, digs the ground, looks at it, puts the bone back, buries it and then, gets it out again and finally eats it, sometimes the whole bone in one go, sometimes bits at a time. Your karmas are these old bones; your old bones are just that, you need to look at them. Bury them for a little while until you feel ready to digest them all. You need to really respect your bones/karma and let yourself transcend yourself totally in embracing them. Old large bones are old karma; they cannot be digested in one go. The bones remain forever if not totally released and integrated. The term "skeletons in the closet" is a metaphor for your "bones" carrying such karma. A skeleton reminds you of your past. The fear of observing a skeleton can be overwhelming for students of wisdom.

The Egyptian Museum in Cairo's, "The Mummies Room" is such an example. The contrast emotionally in observing the sacred blue lotus ponds teeming with life and extraordinary magic outside the Cairo museum and seeing the partially wrapped dead Pharaohs is such an example. How dead are the dead when we don't extinguish their bones and don't let them extinguish their own bones? We must not hold onto them because their bones cannot be released. We do the dead a great disservice when we don't *"let their bones go, and rest in peace."*

If you feel you are holding onto or have a deceased person in any form or karmas with loved ones, you may like to explore this intense aspect of lost karma.

Before you begin the following visualization exercise, it is important to give yourself space, free from your mind. Be aware of your breath; breathing in deeply, powerfully and rhythmically.

You may like to experience this visualization energetically if you are grieving for a lost loved one.

Release Visualization

Open your deceased loved one's ashes container (buried or cremated it does not matter) to look at them and release yourself from them and your life with this person. Observe the fragments of their bones, tiny shards of brittle bone among the ashes. Feel them and allow these bones to disappear. They must be allowed to disappear. The feeling to release them and the person after your journey with them begins your own reclaiming of your new identity.

The most painful karmas are stored in the bones. They are dense and weighty, and they are very immobile. Your own relationship with your body's bones is a very good example. Search your bones' history. Where do you store joint pain? Where have you broken bones? Your spinal column is such an important reminder of your blue print as a human. It has so much stored memory. Your spinal column is a data house of stored memory as it holds pain. Atmospheric conditions such as cold weather, etc. affect the spinal column. It feels the atmospheric pressure and releases the stored memories to the body.

Feel the bones in the head. They encase the brain. The skull is ethereal. Look at a skull. It is death. Examine a skull and feel your own death. Examine your dental records. Intimate reminders of your history are karmically stored in the bones.

Breathe deeply now and ask The Keepers of The Mysteries of the Divine Feminine to reveal to you the relationship you have with your bones in deep release work. Which part of my anatomy structurally is the karma the memory stored?

Trace an outline of your karma with your bones' stored memory. In doing this myself I felt it in my heart area. Firstly I scanned my whole body and felt pressure in the pelvis, heart, neck and head, and left arm. *So which area do I concentrate on?* I was guided by The Keepers to go to the heart and was told that bones carry trauma; they are absorbers of great shock and trauma; they are the shock absorbers and while they may not have been crushed themselves they just carry the load of trauma dumped into the tissues (muscles, etc.)

Allow yourself to release this periodically.

This deep release work is very important to do regularly especially when you have a bone problem. When you next have a bone ache remember The Keepers are able to contact the source of this pain and release it for you. You need to feel the freedom of just allowing this to take place. The Keepers are the custodians of all aspects of bone pain. The bone and its marrow are transmitters of energy throughout the body. Ask The Keepers to help you in this way. Your life reveals this stored memory.

Bringing The Mysteries to you is a journey of self-knowledge. Your knowledge bank is the blue print for the consciousness of your own creation. The creation is NOW about your truth. Allowing yourself to really grow this new part of yourself is already implanted in your cellular memory.

All memory needs is activation of the brain stem. The brain stem stimulates the cortex of cell memories. Place your hands on your brain stem at the back of the head. You will begin to allow for the activation process to take place. This space is one of absolute power for your understanding of how the treatment outcome will be. The brain stem activates the cells in the cortex of the brain and tiny transmitters are fed into the blood stream and the memory bank becomes activated. It is at this point that the breakthrough appears and you need to feel that you are able to go back into these stored memories and release them, so you can free the patterns in the body which keep recurring, lifetime after lifetime. Just releasing all patterns of stored fear will bring much suppression to the surface and you will experience powerful release. This release work is extremely cathartic, very fast and powerful.

Entering through the Gates

My relationship with The Keepers deepens daily as I bring them into healings and my personal life while writing. An extraordinary synchronicity happened in relation to The Keepers' presence in my life. I had read Wallis Budge's book "The Egyptian Book of the Dead," but for some unknown reason couldn't connect with his translation (perhaps it was the actual translation energy by this crusty British patriarchal Egyptologist or the historical context). For two months I put out for another user-friendlier version to deepen my relationship with The Keepers. There just seemed to be an itch that wouldn't go away. As usual the "universe" provides if needed. A good friend who is an artist and teacher provided the link. He saw a vision of an Egyptian female being with arms outstretched, tattoos across her upper body and arms "quite luscious and gob smacking" was his physical reaction to the being. The Egyptian female being told him to take his personal book by Thomas George Allen, "*The Book of the Dead*" (Allen 1974) and give it to me. The being just literally told him (at 3:00 in the morning) to take it off the shelf and what's more, get that brass ankh which had just arrived from Cairo as a gift to him and give it to me also.

This friend is a rare book collector as well as professional illustrator in the media; the vision was so strong and real to him that he felt compelled to obey instructions immediately.

I had been channeling a being through my "High Priestess" transmissions; however, I didn't know if she was the same being my friend had in his vision. I requested him to draw her immediately when he gave me the book and ankh. The stunning illustration from my friend reinforced my earlier relationship with her in a sketch I channeled of her. She has been with me for a long time and oversees my writing and the collection of information for this book and others.

I believe the spells in "The Book of the Dead" (Allen 1974) are a link to strengthen The Mysteries for my life and work. This was reinforced when a man walked into my healing center. He had never had a healing of any sort, and I sensed he didn't really know why he was here. During the healing he spontaneously begins reciting spells from "The Book of the Dead." To say I was stunned is an understatement. He has been studying and living the Osirian myth in his life and he embodies the Seth Vibration. The journey continues with "The Book of the Dead."

"The Book of the Dead" was proving a catalyst for this journey, and I was in it and didn't know where exactly it was taking me. By allowing myself to explore The Mysteries through the spells as the spells seem to be a "knock on the door," I am just opening to this now and the opportunity to connect with the magic of what The Keepers are offering is all around me. You may like to acknowledge yourself now as a custodian of The Mysteries by reading "The Book of the Dead" and feeling the language in translation. The language of translation is very important to feel. For example I opened a page spell 52, (c), (o),

"...door keeper of him who addresses his land, open to me, open wide to me, make way for me. That I may sit where I will."

There are many doorways. There are many initiations as we make our way into The Mysteries. It's like going deeper and deeper into yourself, into your core, and the spells show The Keepers that you know the gods and goddesses.

Really you are saying:
"I am not a stranger, I come knowing who you are, I knock on your door in my innocence and purity and humility. I come in love for meeting The Keepers."

The Keepers are like bodyguards at a club. The guard looks at you, mentally asking: *"Who are you? Are you dressed appropriately?"* All seems OK. You have the password. You already know the rules. You are a member; you have read the rules, now you must just feel confident in yourself to go through the doorway. This is what the spells were teaching me. We are allowed to embrace The Mysteries of the Divine Feminine; few of us know what we want from our lives. To know what you want from life makes the abundance easier to get.

Ask yourself: *"What do I want from The Mysteries exactly?"*

It is a good time right now to just ponder this.

"What do I want from The Mysteries right now?"

Write to yourself in your journal:
For my life right now I want The Mysteries to give me a sense of completeness in everything.

When you say:
"This is a mystery to me, I don't understand what is happening in my life right now."

This in itself is a sense of completeness.

You may like to intone after taking a long cleansing breath:

"In my life right now I need completeness in this particular area."

You need to list the areas of your life where you need completeness. Is it relationships? Career? Finances? Health? or any other area of your life where you feel there is an aspect that is incomplete. You need to feel that The Keepers of The Mysteries of the Divine Feminine are there for you as you journey inward to bring to your life all that you need for your journey.

This is a time to evoke The Keepers as you have your password or members ticket to get you through the gateway. Confidence in knowing what you want and humility in acknowledging this is very important right now. You need now the freedom to explore The Mysteries and really allow yourself completeness in your journey, as you know what you want from The Keepers.

You go to the club. You want something that club brings you. You now need to know exactly what you want!

Do you know exactly what you want from The Keepers?

What do you need to let go of to get what you want?

Something has to go, there has to be a letting go to gain anything in existence. Everything in existence has a price and this is surrender.

What do I have to surrender in myself for this to happen?

List what you want.

List what you will have to surrender, i.e. you may want a new relationship. What do you have to surrender?

I have to surrender my fear of betrayal in relationships to bring a new relationship to me.

To bring love to you is the demand of being human. The hardest thing in being human is the challenge to love. To really love is the most demanding and horrifying thing for a human, so you need to knock on The Keepers' door to be shown love. The human cannot survive without it, yet shuns it when it comes her way. She cannot see that she needs the very thing she hates so much. There is an absolute hatred of living through the self. Even in grieving there is a hatred of the self. There is hatred in it. There is hatred when it is presented to you. Now let that hatred go.

You are aware of the energy around you that controls the forces of existence. You can see that you don't have very much actual control over what you want in your world. You are now striving in this relationship with yourself in reading this book to bring about the changes required for your journey of truth and trust in yourself for mastery of your desires and fears. You know that your desires and fears equate with one thing. The survival of the little self. The little self wants recognition and pleasure. You are competing with your inner child all the time as she cries and screams for attention to be heard. You need validation for your journey in trust with yourself as you bring home your truth to The Keepers. You leave your struggles at the door. This is important. This is needed. Your needs now need to be examined as you create a new way of exploring your relationship with The Keepers because they are showing you already what you have already learned about yourself. You need to feel responsible for only what you currently have, not anything of the past. The past creates barriers.

To arrive at The Keepers' gateway needs surrender. This surrender of expectations is very important for your life of trust in your journey. Right now, just let go and wait empty to create the new.

Total surrender of all expectations from The Keepers must be allowed now. You must evoke everything you wish for being in alignment for your absolute Divine truth and nothing else, because there will be a karma to process along the way. The absolute Divine truth must be a knowing that in the surrender there is hope and peace for our journey. Peace and hope for your journey is in the surrender to your absolute Divine truth. Being in this state of divinity is very important for you now, as you create your absolute Divine truth in everything you do with The Keepers of The Mysteries of the Divine Feminine.

Allowing the surrender is the greatest gift you can ever give yourself because you are the gift and you need to recognize that the gift and yourself are one. You need to focus now on yourself as being able to surrender by visualizing yourself going into the great nothingness and letting go for all previously held expectations of what surrender is exactly.

Exactly what is surrender?

I surrender to you now.

I surrender in love to you now.

I am one in the surrendering.

I am one in the true surrendering process with you now, as we create in oneness together.

Your surrender to Divine order takes place as you acknowledge that you are one with truth, and oneness for all. The gift of surrender is the surprise of accepting at that moment there is an alchemy, a trust and a knowing that "you" are capable of absolutely nothing, absolutely nothing, no mind, no thoughts. Imagine yourself doing a sky diving jump. In the leap from the plane there must be surrender! Why? What's in it for me? It is not uncommon for some people to take a sky dive when they reach a milestone, say 40th birthday, etc. Why? The desire for the outcome must be greater that the fear of maybe dying if the parachute doesn't release and you crash to your death.

It is the same with your fears. Just allowing yourself to go beyond this fear creates a freedom and an abandonment, which creates strength in you to keep doing these fear-releasing energies.

Just surrender to you.

Just go to you now.

You are free.

You are one.

You are able to find within yourself acknowledgment about yourself you didn't have before.

To arrive at The Keepers' doorway and require admittance demands a great deal from you because you are leaving so much behind. There is so much that must go, because a resurrection requires a stripping away of existing patterns of belief and old attitudes. It is worth the sacrifice because you already have come so far in just getting this far in your life. You need to just find within yourself your own trust in your essence, your individuality, your love of yourself to climb into yourself and really merge with "you." You. You. You. It is always you and it always will be. There is no one else, only "you." No one is as important as yourself as you surrender.

The quest is "you." The quest is the vision of completeness and utter peace in the journey. The descent allows you to explore your primordial fears, which are located in your base chakra, your self-nurturing center and you must first climb down the ladder into your storehouse of fears. The descent cannot begin until the foundations are strong. You must have strong foundations to build a new life.

Let's begin.

You love yourself enough to go into yourself already. Your heart is brave. It trusts itself enough to begin the descent into your own storehouse of fears, located in this energy center.

The base chakra controls the fear around security, particularly in relation to karmic fears and early stored childhood memories.

It is here that you are diving deep within yourself. Many memories are suppressed. It's easy to bury childhood misery, including birth trauma, conception and your life in your mother's womb.

These fears are collected and control the functioning of the lower part of your body. See the energy center as having a trap door.

This trap door can reveal many things you have forgotten or don't wish to retrieve. It is a door of traps and you now need to invite all those who were part of this period of your life to step forward now. Just see the first person appear.

Close your eyes; breathe deeply, powerfully.

You have the trap door cord. The first person, event or memory will challenge your previously held belief about yourself.

Give yourself time to process this exercise.

It can be a long one and will need repeating many times.

Look at who steps onto your trap door now.

Ask yourself now:
"Do I need to release this person from the role he/she played in my life?"

You now need to pull the trap door cord and see the person exit through the door. Just let the person (or event, etc.) go. Don't analyze why he/she has appeared or the memory surfaced in the first place.

You must go to your heart for this exercise. Your heart will tell you to let this person go. This person may have represented a security figure in your life.

This person was your first link with security, i.e. parents, caregivers, etc. Release now. Just let go.

You will need to do this again and again, maybe the person who you need to release, say someone who is a father figure, can keep coming back.

Continue the release work. Just let go.

Ask The Keepers of The Mysteries of the Divine Feminine now to clear out the memory and the result it has had on your belief system. You need not to analyze. It is important to just go within and let go. This visualization will support your release.

Before you begin the following visualization exercise, it is important to give yourself space, free from your mind. Be aware of your breath; breathing in deeply, powerfully and rhythmically.

The Red Room Visualization

Your old lodging house of fears needs release. The first door through the gateway to your absolute Divine Truth can leave you feeling empty. Do not concern yourself. This is normal. Observe over the next 24 hours any dreams and listen to your body telling you just what this energy center is doing to you.

In this visualization try and see yourself in the Red Room. The Red Room is any shade you can imagine. You may also feel black or any dark color. Just see yourself in this space receiving clearing and energy from this space. This space is in the base chakra. You can call it "The Red Room."

I am now in the "Red Room."

Stay here for as long as you need and request that The Keepers of The Mysteries of the Divine Feminine be made available to you for clearing. Just request that this be taking place now.

"I request that The Keepers of The Mysteries clear from my cellular memory, all memories, events, traumas located in my Red Room."

Now see which Keeper operates on you.

Bring your consciousness to your Red Room. You are at your base chakra in your Red Room, self-nurturing center.

For the next 24 hours honor yourself and carefully diarize exactly where you may have been feeling vulnerable in areas which relate to core security in your life. You need to really examine and attend to any emotional reactions that spring from this relationship you're developing with yourself.

This exercise may make you feel empty and alone. You may not like the feeling of being alone in this space. You may feel very vulnerable as though something is going to leap out behind the black curtains you have placed around your Red Room. Your Red Room could be seen as a stage. You may see yourself lying on a healing table feeling alone, like waiting for an operation to begin. It feels very empty. Lack of security means aloneness, emptiness for you in the Red Room of your base chakra.

Clear all your energy center rooms regularly. Go into your Red Room and stay there for as long as you wish and bring to yourself your truth. Re-create your Red Room over a 24-hour period for as long as you need to bring clearing and peace to this space.

Offer The Keepers a small gift for healing you in your Red Room. (A gift of rose and musk oil anointed on your hands and lower body.)

In doing this visualization myself, I found flames licking the red curtains. I felt the room had become an undertaker's waiting room, and I was in a coffin. The flames got larger, more fiery. I could hear the roar and they enveloped my dead body. My body became white ash after the fire had gone.

Forming a relationship with The Keepers of The Mysteries of the Divine Feminine is a special responsibility to your sacred truth and you must journal and witness your emotional states for some time afterward.

The creative life, which develops from your relationship with yourself, will really begin to take off. Your creativity is your sacred self expressing itself and your creative self is kept trapped in your base chakra. If you are suppressing yourself for the sake of security through others, this is a time to free the creative self and really explore your passion for release here. There may be a need to feel the power and force of the Sa Sekhem Sahu (the Ancient Egyptian term for the Kundalini) or Kundalini energy awaken in you, this force is also known as the spirit of fire, the serpent of creation.

Your base chakra is the foundation for everything that you experience because all life cannot take form without this center humming. Feel the energy of it humming gently in your body right now. The hum and throb of it creates in you a resonance with your primordial instinctual power and the great Sa Sekhem Sahu is awakened. Be very gentle with yourself. Don't bring too much visualization to this experience of awakening the Kundalini until you are ready. Be alive to the energy of transformation. This is your transforming time.

Awakening the humming center can be a dangerous exercise for some, so you must be aware of the forces you will unleash as you unveil the most sacred of centers, the base chakra. Breathe now into the Earth and take the energy down to the core of the Earth and be anchored first.

Before you begin the following visualization exercise, it is important to give yourself space, free from your mind. Be aware of your breath; breathing in deeply, powerfully and rhythmically.

The Red Room and Serpent Visualization

See the base chakra (self-nurturing center) as a basket with a serpent in it. If you shake the basket "all hell breaks loose." The serpent spits, hisses, bites and attacks. The serpent forces its way through your energy centers causing destruction and bringing up all unresolved issues in your life.

Approach the basket carefully and ask yourself:

"What do you want from the serpent?"

Look at the serpent.

Form a relationship with it.

It is you. Get to know it: as yourself.

You are safe with your serpent if you treat it with respect.

You are in your Red Room now.

Sit with your legs folded in yoga position, breathe love into this center. Breathe energy into it now. Breathe peace into it now.

Evoke The Keepers of The Mysteries of the Divine Feminine now as you gently explore your sacred, secret self. You are on a journey of inner discovery. You are now free to embrace yourself as you create love for yourself in this space. This is the center of death. It is No. 13 in the Tarot. (The Death Card.) Death in this center is the grim reaper, the stalker, the ghoul and the destroyer. Meet the challenge of death as you knock on The Keepers door of your Red Room.

To be afraid of death is to be afraid of life. Death is the grim reaper, the skeleton. Why are we so afraid of our bones stripped bare, naked? Our bones are our fears, because all of our protective coverings are gone. Study a picture of a skeleton. The Mummy's Room in the Cairo museum is one of the most graphic examples I can illustrate. Varanasi (the city of the dead) in India is another example where I have witnessed the burning Ghats cremation ceremonies on the Ganges River. Day after day I arrived at dawn in the crematorium Ghats studying my own reaction to these "skull smashing" ceremonies, as the fluids in the deceased's head exploded like a cannon.

Now imagine yourself in The Mummy's Room in Cairo museum and visualize all those dead pharaohs, their beauty, power and life force stripped bare and naked, with their bones revealed for all to see under the waxy coverings of the mummy's linen. Observe their ghoulish faces, eyeless sockets and grinning mouths.

Challenge and defy your fears; go to your "skeleton" now.

"What are you fearful of in your own skeleton? What skeletons are in my closet now?"

Go to your closet. Look at your skeletons. The Keepers are the custodians of the secrets of the universe, so they are able to help you resurrect your fears and they are willing to assist in the recovery of your lost self. Your lost self is in the wilderness, and you as a human have created a form, a body, to uncover these parts of yourself. Your relationship with The Keepers just keeps getting stronger and stronger as you go into the secret self. Your secret self creates a space for this inner exploration to take place safely and with humility for what you will discover about yourself.

As you breathe gently and lovingly for yourself, redecorate your Red Room and turn it to the most beautiful example of what you can for this energy center. Begin now. Re-gut it. Decorate it and begin the construction of what you want this secure room to look like.

Evoke the senses.

"What do I see, hear, taste, touch and smell in my Red Room?"

Really create a sacred space within yourself to reclaim your lost identity in your Red Room. Create it by visualization.

Using the five primary senses: Allow yourself to see, hear, touch, taste and smell, your Red Room's interior.

List all the attributes you want for your Red Room in your base chakra now.

This exercise is very important for re-claiming your identity with yourself.

Your identity is now being honored and treated with respect. Allow yourself to do this now. Bring all energy centers in a state of resonance with your Divine Truth and you will have created a sound relationship with your own security. See this taking place within you consciousness now.

I am alive to the sense of oneness, as I see, hear, taste, touch and smell my new self. All of me is in celebration now as I come home to my base chakra's Red Room.

Give yourself love and peace now as you have created this sacred center and made yourself secure. You will find there is a sense of peace and wholeness in your relationship with this energy center. This energy center is now being prepared to strengthen you for your ascension upward. The journey upward now will commence with the red center fully secure. It is impossible to build a house without firm foundations, because the structure just collapses to the ground.

You must reinforce this "security" center every day. Every day there must be attention to this energy center. This energy center is one of great power; it is a big red furnace and must be fueled with loads of energy daily.

See it as being like a ship's furnace.

The fuel must be kept up for it to keep alight.

You need now to create such an energetic space now for your furnace by the type of fuel you give it.

The fuel for your power center is breath and visualization.

Visualization must be from the Earth. Much energy comes to this chakra from the Earth. The Earth now is the truth for this center.

Visualize the red Earth, the great red Earth creating fuel with your breath for this center daily.

The daily task must be to fuel this center.

Try and feel the love and energy creating power in you now.

You need to feel the power creating strength in the lower part of your body and just feel the power of your new creation. This is a time to surrender and trust in yourself as you journey in. This is a time to create energy and power as you bring to your life your power to know you are capable of love and truth for yourself.

Bring to your red center your love and your heart. Bring your heart to your center now.

Your newly created Red Room now awaits you. Fill your Red Room with something new now. (Perhaps a red ruby crystal, or red lava from volcanoes, etc.)

Death is one aspect of this center; birth is another.

In my early energy work with this center I had a panic attack reliving my own traumatic birth when swimming and doing breath work every day. I really had to examine birth as a form of death too, it felt easy to die and watch my corpse be destroyed but birth was a different matter. It was very hard.

I also energized this center through a mountain climb, doing a meditation on the summit.

During this deep exploratory work you may find your dreams quite challenging. I found my dreams were of me being alone, in deserts, strange tombs, bones everywhere, night after night.

Allowing the forces of nature to assist in the process of reclaiming your identity is very important for your energy work with these centers. Our relationship with the natural forces in nature must be honored and trusted, and you need to feel the connection with these sacred forces daily. You need to really embrace the natural elements into your everyday world and bring their essence into your totality daily. You cannot re-claim your absolute Divine truth, without evoking the forces of nature to assist you, and create with you in love and trust for your truth. Give yourself a break in nature daily and merge with these forces for your journey now. Give your whole body and spirit a renewal with the sacred forces of nature. Merge with them as you go within to create all you need for your truth and oneness with all.

This strengthens your Red Center; brings you close to the Earth. Give yourself now the feeling of All Love and peace.

The Keepers are aware that in creating a space of forgiveness for yourself to believe in your truth is a great leap, bringing great power to you now, as you create in oneness with The Mysteries. The Mysteries are just that; they are a recreation of your own power and love for yourself. Your relationship with The Mysteries is your relationship with yourself. The trust and belief in yourself is your greatest gift to yourself and your greatest gift in being human right now. To create The Mysteries one must have a simple faith in being able to cross the boundary into your power and truth for yourself. Your life must be one of supreme sacrifice to yourself.

You must sacrifice yourself to yourself as you re-create The Mysteries within yourself now. The Divine being you are is "yourself" and your "truth." There is no other way The Mysteries create in you a living relationship with your truth and your abundance. Your abundance is related to your truth. You cannot have one without the other and you cannot create from a space of fear. You need to re-create from a space of abundance, not fear, not denial. This is your truth right now. This is your belief in your truth right now. To create love in abundance brings you closer to The Mysteries as they are all around you. Your knowledge of The Mysteries is your inner exploration of yourself. Your inner exploration of you in your totality. Live this now, feel this now.

To create The Mysteries in your own life you must live a life of truth and surrender. To surrender is the greatest learning a human must undergo and there is no other way to experience bliss, peace and immortality. You must endeavor to practice surrender and observe small surrenders every day.

Every day practice a small surrender.

"What do I need to surrender today?"

Ask yourself, *"Where is my surrender now?"*

"What must I surrender today?"

To surrender implies in our human society, weakness and lack of strength. Actually, the most ennobling thing a human can do is to surrender. To surrender to the enemy in war is to wave the white flag of surrender. This surrender becomes an acknowledgment, not of weakness, but a willingness to give up control over a desired outcome. The white flag becomes a symbol of purity of release and the "winners" are traditionally benevolent toward the surrendering enemy.

To surrender gives power and freedom. I surrender to you doesn't mean I am weaker than you, but I trust myself enough in love to really re-claim freedom over myself.

I re-claim my freedom over myself through the loving act of surrendering to a Higher Force, that I acknowledge, to protect me.

I am surrendering to myself actually an aspect of myself who is able to feel freedom in truth. I am free when I can do this.

The art of surrender is the next step in attaining your own power over your relationship with yourself. This time is one of absolute surrender in the Divine sense. The art of surrender is the most powerful expression of your own essence. It is as if your essence is yours now for the first time. The essence of your truth is your ability to really connect and be a part of the totality of your humanness right now. The joy of surrender cannot be over emphasized. The absolute joy of true surrender is an exquisite expression of yourself, and you are now in the process of experiencing this right now.

Believing in yourself and your surrender as an art form and as a power statement of your totality is an admission of the absolute love you have for yourself and the forces assisting you at this time. The truth of your trust in yourself must be explored and expressed right now, so your ability to find and create "you" in surrender now is part of "you." Experiencing your totality without attachment, being in the essence of yourself is being in the essence of your truth for yourself right now.

Create, create, create.

To create the art of surrender is believing in the joy of "this" moment, this exquisite second, to create in you, your truth.

The Keepers are the surrender creators.

The Keepers of The Mysteries of the Divine Feminine actually create the surrender process.

The surrender is part of the journey for your spiral upward. Your energy belt ascension begins with the base chakra (self-nurturing center).

Ask yourself, *"What do I have to surrender in my base chakra now?"*

Your base chakra contains the blue print for your incarnation in a primitive society. Your primitive brain reacts to this craving for security by recreating the cave energy and the need for security. Surrendering this fear creates the change in the structure of your base chakra; your Red Room.

In a meditation you may like to intone:

"I now must surrender my security, my base chakra fears, from all incarnations in all lifetimes, in the name of love and light and my absolute Divine Truth."

Now that the chakra's energy field is fully cleared and surrendered, I am now able to open up to balancing and clearing all energy centers in my holographic body.

My body is a holography of my emotions and my spirit. My body must be strong and powerful to take the charge. My emotions and spirit self are calling for change.

"Can my body take this charge?"

"Can I survive the challenge of such powerful change?"

Surrendering creates such a powerful challenge to change your base chakra reality.

It is from this point that you can begin the climb, the ascension through the chakras. The ascension through the chakras takes place when your relationship with your ability to surrender has been achieved. The Keepers are initiating you right now, as you create through them your power and truth in this center.

Where is the best place energetically for you to spiritually surrender "for yourself" to the energy of this chakra?

You need to go to a "cave or a womb-like" place, preferably a dark space (not light); total blackness if possible. Refer to my book "The Alchemies of Isis Embodiment through The High Priestess" (Glenane 2016) for "Dark Moon" information. See if you can go into nature at night. Perhaps you can camp in a tent in the wilderness or a cave in the mountains. The tombs in the Valley of the Kings, in Egypt, are another place I have explored for this powerful energetic work, as well as caves in Peru and Turkey.

On a teaching tour to Egypt I asked my students to do this core energetic work while alone. Anubis was invited to protect their journeys. They were to meet a High Priestess to guide them to this secret dark place within themselves, in one of the tombs alone. Each student experienced an intense emotional release, in this surrender.

Find an evening alone in nature where you can do this work, go through the sequence and be familiar with what you are requesting. Dark moon would be a perfect time. Record your experiences; remember you are clearing your self- nurturing center and surrendering.

The love The Keepers of The Mysteries of the Divine Feminine have for you is endless, and you must feel free now to really create exactly what The Keepers want for your energetic journey with them. Remember the holograph. You are the holographic, and the holographic blue print you have creates a resonance with The Keepers to respond. It is as though you have the key lock combination in your head and The Keepers are now trying out different key combinations to unlock your codings to awaken your inner self. You must again surrender and must trust the forces assisting you right now in your time of struggle.

There is a struggle going on internally and the struggle relates to your ability to grasp what you have to let go of and release. This is an adjustment in your reality and there is always a struggle. Imagine now just surrendering so you can allow The Keepers to do their job for you now.

Creating peace in the process of surrendering is essential for your journey now. Your journey creates the challenge of just connecting to peace. Surrender brings peace. Surrender brings self love. Allow. Allow. Allow. The spirit of surrender is the essence of being human and the essence of a peace-filled life.

There are so many levels and layers in the surrender process and just being aware of them is very important for your journey right now. Acknowledging to yourself what you have to surrender today creates a space and framework for your journey. A framework for the process of surrender releases you from fear and control of others in your life. This is a time to recognize that surrender is very important for you to review The Mysteries. The Mysteries cannot be revealed if you do not surrender.

When you empty out the "backpack" of life very day, you are surrendering.

During your evening meditation you may like to intone:

"I want to continue my walk on my road to freedom. Now I must stop and let go. I must give myself a change to lighten my load.

Do this now.

"What weighs me down in life at the moment?"

"Where do I feel the most weight?"

"Where is the most weight in your life?"

Find it in your body, i.e. where does your body carry weight or pain, etc.?

Where is the tension?

This part of your body carries the tension of accumulated pain, fear and loss. When this is released you have surrendered some part of yourself that has been weighing you down.

Check your body. Scan it, feel where the pain is stored. Now let The Keepers release this load.

All doors to The Keepers reveal different aspects of the self, the "self" that needs reclaiming.

The reclamation of the "self" is the "self" service to the "self."

The "self" serves the "self" and is re-creating the "self" every day.

I serve the "self" in many large and small ways every day.

As I re-claim myself, my reclamation of myself is truly the gift of love for me right now as my identity and essence is in the reclaiming "self."

The "self" creates the most powerful relationship in being human and that is allowing the mystery to unfold. The essence of being human is in the discovery of the "self," the true "self" is now the essential and only truth you must carry. You need now to really feel the essence and wisdom of the self and the essence and wisdom of the self is the art of the Feminine. It is the Feminine principle. The Feminine principle is in the Mystery. All Feminine is in the Mystery. The Sacred Feminine: The Mystery.

The Sacred Feminine Mystery is the essence of the human spirit. Allowing the Mystery of life to be part of your essence now is an initiation. This initiation is now allowing you to create in you a true sense of oneness with all there is. This time to create with the Sacred Feminine is now one of peace and allowance of the self to be the self and to acknowledge the Mystery being an essentially Feminine thing.

The Keepers are initiating you now. As you read this is to be initiated by The Mystery. The Mystery is just the layers, the unfolding you are experiencing now as you prepare for the undertaking of your next journey.

We have to initiate you now.

We have to create now.

Intone now:
"I am in a sacred space of creation."

"I am one with sacred creation. I allow sacred creation to take place now. Really I am now in a profoundly sacred creative space in my essence right now."

"I am one. I am all."

The Mystery of the Divine Feminine is in the sacredness of all life. You must not see any part of your life as being different or more special. This creates separation and division. The sacredness of the Feminine, the pure sacredness is purely a Feminine undertaking. The purity of the Feminine is the sacred Divine Feminine, the pure sacred Divine Feminine lies in "The Now." The pure essence, the absolute pure essence of it is in "The Now." You are a product of "The Now." The sacredness of "The Now" is in you.

So the purity of "The Now" is in the sacred Feminine Mysteries.

The purity of "The Now" is in the codings you have come to Earth with, but these codings have become damaged and interfered with and they are not even being used any more. You need to feel the energy, love and truth of your life being one with the immortal ones as you open up your world to create new mysteries. The Mysteries of creation are in the sacredness of your own spirit self and these writings; these sacred writings must be evoked by you now in truth for who you are.

It is just so simple to live a lie and to create nothing.

What is creation anyway?

Why not create a new "self"; a new sacred Divine Feminine "self."

Give yourself a "makeover."

"I am going to create a new me. It is called the 'Divine Feminine' me."

This is the recipe for the makeover; your transformation begins right now.

Just empty yourself of everything. A room must be bare for it to be re-decorated. Now strip back all your old layers, starting with your body. You cannot bring new furniture into a room when it is full of clutter, so begin now. I now begin my transformation,

Now look at your body: Strip it, look at yourself nude. Really take it and look at what you have to renovate. X-ray your bones; The Keepers always are reminding you that your bones are your history. Your karma is stored in your bones and vertebrae.

Look at stiffness of your joints.

Are you flexible? Is there pain in bones?

"What do I need to do to reclaim in my relationship with my skeletal structure?"

Breathe new life into your bones, now. Really breathe new life into your marrow.

Feel the light, like a laser light being infused into the marrow. Your marrow's function is to make blood. Create the opportunity to make your marrow, strong healthy, full of life and energy.

Your relationship with your bones must come next, straight after the marrow workout. Examine major problems with your teeth: root fillings, extractions, etc. The external reminder of how you care for yourself through your teeth and bones must be considered. You must allow the life force to be infused to all this creation. Really creating the mystery of your life through examining your body is the most wonderful relationship you can have with yourself.

Begin to just feel the essence of creation within yourself now. You need to really feel that the power of your body is the power of being in the "now." The body is a machine for everything that is in your life and you cannot be spiritual and explore a relationship with your Divinely Feminine self until your body is as perfect as you can get it. The body must be maintained daily with body stretches, yoga, exercise and daily attention. Allow it to talk to you. Really form a relationship with it as you create a new body for yourself. I am creating a new relationship with my body, and I may bring in to my life a relationship with all of life through my body. Allow your body to be part of your essence and who you are. Breathe freedom into it.

We get old when our bodies cannot do all the things they need to. So, create your new body. You may need to employ some person to help you to this, i.e. personal trainer, yoga teacher, body harmony trainer, etc.

Establishing a relationship with breath as a living force is essential. Breathe in to the count of eight – hold to the count of eight – release to the count of eight – pause. Now deepen your connection and earth yourself with the breath as you observe the flow of breath into the meridians and chakras, and feel the flow of breath really drenching all of your cells, going right into your core identity.

Really create a new model in your humanness and don't allow any previously held belief about yourself to create in you anything that is not for the highest intent. Your energy, love and life force must remain detached from your emotions and mind and love-filled at all times. All of life is an embrace of the core part of yourself and this core part of you is the fluid, the marrow inside your bones. The marrow is responsible for flow of life force, prana in your body.

Visualize yourself in your skeleton. Imagine the large bones, feel inside them. Imagine what happens to the bones when the marrow does not nourish the bones feeding them with vital nutrients and body-building enzymes. The bones can break or fracture. Visualize yourself recoding your marrow. Recode your marrow to accept new frequencies, i.e. activation of your Mt DNA for rejuvenation –refer to my book "Awaken your Immortal Intelligent Heart" (Glenane 2016). Imagine the gelatin-like liquid. Visualize gelatin; gelatin sets jelly, it makes liquid set.

You can re-set your relationship with how your body responds to anything. Imagine all those stored karmas, sitting in your cells, responding to stimuli. The karma responds to stimuli for example: a film, a face, a song, a memory, a touch activates karma, either positive or negative.

Now flood the cells with this new strengthening life force through the gelatinous structure of the marrow, to change your cellular memory, bringing in this new strengthening life force. The marrow codings create much energy and power because the cells are being renewed at the core, the beginning of life as we begin as a gelatinous mass before our bones were formed.

It is a most powerful aspect of our own power to regenerate and rejuvenate ourselves that we can go into our own marrow and recode it with The Keepers help. We need to feel as though we have this power and the marrow healings create this through training thought processes. Faulty thought processes create disease in the first place.

Even before our bones are formed, we are pure liquid, which is composed of marrow. This marrow is the nucleus of our life and the marrow holds the key to creation as we can re-create ourselves through our marrow. You need to feel the energy, magic and essence of creation in the marrow as you journey into an unknown part of your own cellular history. The marrow begins the journey of life and is affected by all around it. It is particularly susceptible to vibration and sound so you need to allow the essence of vibration to be one with the energy of marrow. Crystal sound bowl healing is very effective. The feeling of marrow healing can resonant all around your body (i.e. you may like to imagine you are in a liquid light gelatin bath). You need to feel the liquid of marrow, having a separate life and intelligence, like a living squid or sea creature. The creatures of the seas are us, and the energy of the oceans and tides affect our marrow, because our marrow resonates primarily to its home the liquid mass, the oceans, waters of life. Allowing yourself time to resonate with the moving living creatures in the oceans wakes up our marrow to its original intention to create life and sustain life.

Marrow sustains life and marrow is the regenerator of you. When you allow your marrow to regenerate through the forces of water by allowing it to resonate with the water, you have found a key to the mystery of creation. The mystery of creation lies in the process of oneness and is in the spirit of creation itself. This is the time for us to really see ourselves as being part of the web of life and all of the elements that make up creation can assist, when we who are part of creation are damaged emotionally, physically or at soul level. No one in the world is independent of another and all help when there is an emotional or spiritual or health crisis is given. This is just how it is. The marrow responds to the concept of marrow resonance. In Richard Gerber's book "A Practical Guide to Vibrational Medicine", (Gerber R. 2001) he states that:

"All of the universe responds to a vibration that is not part of the whole. Just as a mother picks up a crying child the universal elemental forces respond to this energy dysfunction."

For this is what crisis is, a dysfunction of energy and if you want to renew yourself in your human form and don't choose to return to elemental forces, yet you must feel and evoke these forces at every level of your being. Just feeling the incredible assistance of all around you creates such power and energy in you. This is time to create your relationship with yourself as you do this and bring to your life your trust in yourself to really go beyond all previously held ideas about your role in your life as being suppressed.

Disease equals suppression. If you have a disease, physical or emotional, you have suppressed all forces assisting you. You must release to allow the sea elementals who can help you. You are not even separate from these elementals.

Allow. Allow. Allow. The secret is in the allowance of yourself. The self must be integrated enough for the allowance to take place and the allowance is in the release. Allow the release to initiate you into The Mysteries. Just allow the release to take place. Just allow the release to be your right. It is a right, a sacred human right to allow this to happen now.
This allowance takes place in you right now.

Allow the mystery to be you.

"I allow myself space to experience the mystery."

"I must allow myself as a human being my potential."

"I must allow my potential to enfold."

"I allow myself this knowing and this acceptance of the now."

The acceptance of the now is in the knowing of the now. The knowing of the now is the moment of realization of the mystery like a conception; the conception takes place in the allowance, in the emptiness, in the allowance of something to come from nothing.

There must be an allowance for this to take place at some level. When you let go of allowing the mystery it becomes enacted once again, as it takes place because of the state of allowance.

The state of allowance is in the mystery.

Allow. Allow. Allow.

Let the mystery begin.

Open the curtain now.

Allow.

Bring to your life right now the surrender, the absolute delicious surrender. Allow the surrender to be sweet surrender. There is a sweetness and purity in surrender. There is that moment, that perfect moment, when it is absolutely bliss. The feeling of the great unknown, the Great Mother, unfolding herself to you. The knowing that you are going to be able to be enclosed in the safety net. The feeling that you are being looked after regardless of what happens. The knowing that something protects you and that you are just safely looked after. This is time now to really concentrate on allowing yourself this safety and surrender and the knowledge that you are above it all and that "you" are now totally free and safe to do exactly what you like for your journey of trust and safety for yourself. There must be a space within you now, which allows this love and energy to be there for you as you explore an unknown part of yourself. This safety and surrender is yours now to embrace totally. Allow the new way of being human to merge with you now in safety and oneness for all. You now need validation and support for your journey as you begin this unknown part of yourself to create in you magic, peace and safety. You are now in a space of suspension and knowing. The suspension now is in the trusting of unknown forces to guide you.

The opportunity to explore all parallel universes is now open to you as you embrace The Keepers' wisdom. This is a time for mergence and oneness and you need to feel the absolute essence of all. The absolute essence of all is yours now as you create in magic and wonder, your truth. The creation of your truth brings your power and magic through The Keepers. You need to feel the simple truth of absolute and Divine surrender. Really there is no other way and your relationship with The Keepers is a mystery in itself, as it will just keep deepening the love you have for yourself. This is a time for this deepening and awakening, and you need to just experience the essence and power of love. This essence and power of love is one for you now as you embrace your humanity with your essence. You are allowing a part of yourself that has been trapped for so long to emerge and you need to feel the essence of your truth really ignite you in oneness and truth for yourself. You are now allowing soul love for yourself to create for you a sense of uniqueness and wonder in your humanness right now. This is a time for you to create in oneness and magic and to really let go and suspend yourself into nothingness. Absolute nothing, absolute nothing for your journey of trust; now you are love.

You are now in a most powerful position in your life, as you have created in your life absolute and Divine surrender to your absoluteness and wonder.

The Mystery you embody is yours now as you feel the strength, love and compassion for your Divine self, which lives in you and creates you.

You now are looking through the doorway. The Key and Ankh (Egyptian symbol for eternal life) have the power you need now to create and embrace The Mysteries. You are the mystery. You are the one and there can be no other in your world. Your world is one of magic now, because there is no tomorrow only now because you right now are the sum total of your universe. Your universe must embrace the sum total of who you are and you in turn must be embraced too. This is a time to embrace your true self and create your true self to really create in love and respect for yourself. The absolute essence of who you are is now part of your totality and your totality must be above all. The energy, essence and oneness of the sacred universe is yours now as you allow the pattern of oneness to merge fully with you. This is a time to really create the sense of wonder and respect for who you are and to allow this sacred essence to be part of you now.

All life is a celebration of your own joy in being human. You need now to create for your life now, the absolute joy, love and wonder embracing and enfolding you now as you are the master magician and you hold the key to your own universe which is all of creation. Because there is no separation and fear, there cannot be destruction. There is no destruction. There is no destruction because there is no fear. Your life is now a creative act of mergence with The Mysteries now. There is only one life. It is yours. The Keepers do not allow just the unveiling of The Mysteries to the uninitiated so you must test the uninitiated, part of your "self." You must feel that the uninitiated part of your "self" is ready for the journey. This is a time to really allow the sacred Mysteries to unfold in you first, because of you.

You are the mystery.

You are the absolute essence of the sacred Mysteries and you need now to acknowledge this to yourself for your unique life of trust and love in yourself.

You are the sacred art.

You are the mystery.

The journey into the heart of yourself creates the pleasure of enlightenment and love for yourself. You need now to bring to yourself The Mysteries through the love of the sacred Mysteries themselves. The Sacred Mysteries themselves just keep re-occurring in a way, which will astound you when you really allow them to be part of you. You need to feel The Mysteries in every living thing and honor The Mysteries in yourself. They are not hard. They are easy. You must surrender to them and you must feel unafraid to really explore and test your own sacredness against The Mysteries. This is a time to really honor The Mysteries in yourself and really bring to your life your sacred universal self. This is a time to believe the sacred

Mysteries as living energies within yourself and create them within and without. This is your journey. You now need to gather the sacred Mysteries within yourself and create them in every way imaginable.

This is your time to just create the sacred Mysteries within yourself and just be with the energies of sacredness within you. You are one with the sacred Mysteries within you and you need to create the sacred mysteries within you now. This is an important aspect of your identity.

You must bring the sacred art of The Mysteries within you by respecting yourself first.

The first introduction to The Mysteries is to the "self."

I am serving the "self" when I serve The Mysteries in me.

I serve myself first, how can The Mysteries become part of me until I serve the "self."

I serve the "self" first and then The Mysteries will be revealed to me.

I serve the "self."

The "self" is The Master.

You cannot serve another until you serve the "self."

The Keepers are always observing you and they will bring now the force of oneness with you as you create with them. The freedom to explore your own inner self is the essence of The Mysteries. The essence of The Mysteries is in the creation of yourself as an artwork. Look at yourself as a piece of artwork. It is perfect and pure of heart. To bring anything less is a denial of yourself and your potential. You need to feel the absolute beauty of yourself as a creative force. To bring yourself to the doorway requires simple trust in yourself that you have done your very best, the absolute very best with what you have in your life now. You really need to experience this in yourself.

Which part of you needs to be made perfect now?

What part of yourself now is needed to create with The Mysteries?

Why, you ask yourself, are you not able to step up the stairs now, to embrace The Keepers?

To be able to look at The Keepers in humility and love for yourself is the most important aspect of yourself.

Don't view yourself negatively. If there is something that hasn't been worked on, you may like to ask yourself these questions.

What isn't really beautiful to yourself, you cannot present it to The Keepers.

Look at what you are offering The Keepers. Don't offer rubbish. Offer the very best you can afford, for it is what we can afford is what is being received. Allow this to happen in you now.

You need to look at yourself before you visit the great Keepers. Drawing on the power of the ancient Egyptian Mystery School traditions can help. The great father Osiris, (Ancient Egyptian God) needs to see you in your humility.

Breathe deeply, powerfully and rhythmically and ask yourself in meditation:
What can I offer now?

What have I made of my life?

What now do I need to seek spiritually which will purify?

You need the essence of giving yourself the very best.

The Keepers are now ready to activate further memories of your life with them. In the temples and other sacred places in nature you may have karmically had initiations and now you re-created The

Mysteries together. The Mysteries are now ready for the emergence into oneness with all of life. The Mysteries are now ready to be re-created again through you. Your special relationship with The Mysteries keeps The Mysteries alive on Earth. The special relationship with yourself and The Mysteries is just that, an extraordinary relationship, of trust and love in the wholeness process.

This is a time to re-create The Mysteries in everyday life.

This is a time to bring The Mysteries to you in a new and magical form, and you will feel the purity and essence for all of life coursing through you now.

Just re-create The Mysteries in everything.

This is a time to bring The Mysteries to you in every living way.

This is the mystery.

You are the mystery when you enact the mystery.

You are the mystery when you create something out of something and you are the mystery when you create daily.

"How can I create the mystery in my life now?"

"How can I be one with the mystery in all of life now?"

"How can I be the mystery?"

You are the mystery now, as you re-create in oneness for all of life. Just feel The Mysteries envelop you now as you create in oneness with The Mysteries in all of life now. Just allow the love of The Mysteries to be you now. You are love.

The mystery just keeps growing in you now as you become the magical energy of the mystery. The magical energy of the mystery is the creation of you in every way imaginable. The way of The Mysteries is the way of truth unfolding. The mystery is just that, a creative adventure. In *"The Secret Garden"*, the author Frances Hodgson Burnett explores desire, fear, abandonment, terror and friendship, developing trust and pure love the two children have for each other in finding "The Secret Garden." (Burnett FH 2000)

You cannot access The Mysteries without the trust and pure love. You just must surrender to nothingness, absolute nothingness in the creative process. The act of creation is in the process of just allowing the mystery to re-create itself. All of life re-creates the mystery. All of life is a mystery. When you realize there are hurdles to The Mysteries, you realize that you can't create with these obstacles. Surrender to be one with The Mysteries now!

The belief in allowing the structures of your life to collapse brings such light to you. You must feel the energy of just receiving the light and opening up to its power in your life now. The creation must be without any previously held definition of what creativity even is. You need now to really bring into alignment the forces of absoluteness in everything. Absoluteness is your best weapon to create in magic and hope for your journey.

The absoluteness is now yours as you embrace the mystery. The mystery to you was the enactment, the enactment of all life. All of life is the enactment of the mystery. Allow the mystery to be enacted through you now as you embrace the sacred mystery of love. It is All Love; all light; all power; All Love.

Creating the absoluteness in the knowing is what The Keepers are showing you now and keeping your power open to yourself for your journey must be always part of your journey. This is time to allow the forces of absoluteness to really re-create in you your belief in your own ability to really control the forces of your life. Your life now offers absolute power and detachment. Your life now with The Keepers is one of enacting and re-creating the sacred Mysteries in all of life. You are the holder now of the wisdom and your are now allowing The Keepers of The Mysteries of the Divine Feminine to re-create with you. You are now bringing them to you in your life.

They are now part of you because you believe in the absoluteness of everything. You believe in the absoluteness of the Divine Feminine now. You just continue to explore the relationship growing with The Divine Feminine guides.

With your absolute Divine Truth you will open up the doorway even further. Don't be afraid to really explore and trust yourself to get the key to your own "secret garden." You now need to feel this in everything you do so you need now to allow the mystery to unfold and create absoluteness in you now. The absoluteness of your life now must make you connect to the sacred Mysteries. You are one with The Mysteries now. You are one and you are free now to enact The Mysteries.

You are feeling the power of The Keepers in your relationship with yourself at the moment and you must remember that you are really allowing yourself to really find the essence of oneness in everything. You are now knowing and expanding a new part of yourself in your relationship with yourself and you need to feel the power essence and magic of the purity required for such an entrance. You are now creating such passion for all of life in the creation of the sacred Mysteries. The sacred Mysteries are forwarding a new aspect in your reality as you re-create with the Great Mother of Light her love and goodness for you. You are now free from distractions. (Emotional distractions will only forward energy that de-powers you.) You need to feel this freedom from emotional distractions. Then you will feel the energy love and magic of oneness in everything now. This is your heritage and spiritual legacy. Just stay pure and smile. Keep structure and simplicity in your life now.

While The Keepers of The Mysteries of the Divine Feminine are in your life you will need to feel and recognize that there will always be darkness around you trying to get control of your soul's purpose and this you must guard. You need to recognize now the power of saying "No." Just saying "No" will ensure that you are protected even more by light. Just say "No." I say "No" to evil, and I say "No" to the dark. You now have the key. You are powerful and you must learn now to just say "No" and guard your Divine Feminine truth. The truth behind you is the key to the immorality of the soul. So in saying "No" you are creating a barrier so you can forward your truth and your light.

Just recognize now.

By intoning:
"I have the key."

"I say 'No' to everything that does not serve my higher purpose in wisdom for my absolute Divine Truth."

"I say 'No' now."

You are now resonating fully with the Divine Feminine principle, which is a respect for all life. Respect for self just comes before anything and respect for your Divine truth must be made available to you now.

You are feeling The Keepers just being in your Divine presence and they will guard and watch your truth and above all they will protect it and you. Don't worry. Protection is always there. Protection and control are always there.

You are now powerful and a force to be reckoned with.

You don't need emotion and negativity creating barriers between you and your absolute Divine truth, so create now your truth.

The Divine ones, The Keepers are everywhere. Watch and be supportive and bring to your life all that you need for your journey of absolute truth. Stay fixed to your truth right now and recognize its power.

You and You are You.

The Keepers of The Mysteries of the Divine Feminine when asking for commitment from you now create in you a sense of wonder and respect for all life as you journey into this part of yourself. You create with the Keepers. You create with them an honoring of the forces of completeness and wonder for all as you become one with all life.

Your identification with the Keepers is resonating with you at a new level as the completeness and wonder for all of creation is one within you now. The knowledge of this merging is with you now at soul level and you are unafraid of identifying with the absolute Divine truth in everything.

You must always release and be aware of the pain of attachment and your identification with attachment. The essence energy and wonder of non-attachment must be part of your essence, wonder and goodness now.

Just feeling the energy and acknowledgment and respect for the process of oneness with The Keepers now is your truth as you create in wonder and respect for all. The energy love and balance of all life now must be yours as you create in wonder for all. The belief in your absoluteness has come about. The Keepers help. You are the projection of The Keepers' intent in the world now as you brave the world you are in. Continue to nourish this presence and respect for all life now.

Divine love and oneness creates your relationship with The Keepers now that all your energies are directed toward a path of integration. This is a time for you to allow the sacred forces to flow through you as you are bringing to your life all you need for your life of wholeness now. You need to find The Keepers' wisdom all around you now as you create with them "All Love." The Keepers of The Mysteries have taught you now to have the purity of the heart for your absolute Divine truth to now really come home to yourself and allow the sacred flame of your heart to ignite in oneness for you right now.

You need to feel the essence of oneness in everything as you create in oneness now. You need to honor the sacred truth every day in your life and you must be prepared to make sacrifices for these truths. You must always honor yourself first and foremost. Because without honoring yourself first you are unable to carry the tradition and respect of all those around you. This is time to bring The Keepers into all parts of your identity now, by allowing the essence of who you are to live through you. Purify and trust for the journey is yours now as you complete an important cycle in your life. You now must honor and cherish yourself above all else. For no one can take from this.

Your time for this transmission has ended as the sacred ones have integrated themselves through you now.

You are one with these sacred energies as you re-create in oneness for all around you.

You are now free. You are free.

You are us. We are you.

You have honored The Keepers, now you will be given The Keepers' gifts.

Thank you.

This is ended.

Their eyes watch you in the dark.

They are The Keepers of The Mysteries.

For some readers who are not used to evoking protection in meditation, you may like to reflect on the following.

Before you begin the following visualization exercise, it is important to give yourself space, free from your mind. Be aware of your breath; breathing in deeply, powerfully and rhythmically.

Anubis Meditation

Anubis is an Ancient Egyptian deity. Portrayed as a jackal-headed dog on a man or jackal form.

Anubis brings to you protection in all areas of life where there is peril. Peril is the state of consciousness perceived by yourself when you are embracing on any new adventure, which could be seen to be dangerous. Any activities to do with nighttime, and danger around nighttime activities are addressed by my vibration. I am there to be your guard dog in dangerous nighttime situations, where you need guarding. No stalkers stalk you when I am around. Put me at the end of your bed when you are disturbed by astral or unfriendly visitors. Ghosts, poltergeist activity will be banished by my vibration. I am able to assist you for your surgery as I take care of your soul, while your body is in an unconscious state.

This is an important time for new discoveries for humans right now. I am available to allow you to explore "new" soul situations, i.e. astral travel and out of body adventures. I will guard souls lost and help bring them home again. I am friendly but do not become familiar with me, as my role is to watch over you and protect you and your property, especially when you are away. I protect children from dangerous situations, and I guard all those in the dying process, so they can be brought to judgment safely. I help when souls have become lost and need to be given direction. I help you get a good night's sleep if you are grieving for a "lost" love one. I am available for travel, and I allow "your" journey to be conducted safely. I am powerful for you when you are lost in any area of your life.

All losses are addressed by my vibration, but keep me especially for nighttime. If you get lost, visualize me to keep you safe. I create a gateway to the realms of spirit. I stop all fear of you being able to open up your consciousness to new ways of looking at life. Loneliness is addressed by me, especially heaviness associated with aloneness at night. Parents with frightened children at night use me, especially before you go out. Your children will be safe with me.

The following meditation will further deepen your understanding of this new consciousness:

The Keepers of The Mysteries of the Divine Feminine Meditation

The Mysteries of the Divine Feminine consciousness create a sense of oneness with all of creation. This vibration anchors the consciousness of the Divine Feminine Mysteries to Earth at this time for restoration and hope for your world. The time now for human consciousness to embrace the ancient mysteries of the Divine Feminine cannot be over emphasized as they represent the forces needed for your planet's survival. You will find a true sense of oneness, not an abstract sense of oneness, but a true oneness with all of creation.

There is a respect for "self" from this energy, because respect for "self" is the truth behind your existence on Earth.

When there is a respect for "self," there is a love and respect for all.

This is a time now for merging with the ancient Feminine Mysteries, which are the alchemy to forward truth for yourself and others.

Where there is no respect for the "self" there can be no love for "self" or others.

Respect for "self" must come before anything else and overrides all other considerations.

You will find this vibration taking care of all considerations where respect for "self" is an issue.

The Keepers keep. This is it, they keep. The secrets are kept. Revealing a secret is a shared sacred trust and The Keepers are revealing the secrets to you the seeker, because "you" have created conditions in your consciousness to create these amazing secrets to be reactivated in you now.

... Their eyes watch you in the dark. They are The Keepers of The Mysteries.

Part Two:
Entering the Portal of the Heart's Secrets

The Heart's Secrets

When you feel your heart as a living intelligence you are witnessing a metamorphosis in consciousness. The metamorphosis in consciousness begins when your intelligence matches the vibration of the heart's intelligence.

This intelligence brings to you now your own capacity to be totally the master of your ship.

Now imagine this:
You are the captain of a ship. As a captain, you must know every single aspect of how your ship's machinery works.

For example; there is engine failure. Why has the engine failed?

You must now allow yourself to assume responsibility, like the ship's captain, for what your heart is capable of.

What is my heart capable of truly?

Why am I "in pain?"

Why do I have a "disease?"

What has broken down and why?

You are "the captain." You have to know first, and then you can delegate responsibility. Today begins a new journey for you. You, "the captain of the ship," has arrived on your ship.

The passengers, crew and staff, confer respect on "the captain." This is the person who must make the final decisions.

Remember the film, "The Titanic," and its sinking. What do you remember about the captain's responsibility when you saw this film? If you have never seen the film, try to imagine how the captain would behave. What did he do when the full horror of the sinking was revealed?

You are now observing your responsibility to your heart and its secrets. Are you prepared for this responsibility? If you are, you are ready for this book's secrets; outlining your heart's secrets to you so you can safely navigate your ship of life.

Right now just surrendering to your new world of self responsibility is the single most important challenge you can give yourself. As humans, you are conditioned to delegate responsibility to others. Your whole social systems are set up this way. Believing in your own heart's capacity to reveal its secrets begins now when you mentally stop delegating responsibility to others to take care of "it" for you.

Your capacity now is to allow this challenge to present itself to you in various ways. For example, I have accepted responsibility for my heart's totality in revealing answers to me about all aspects of my humanness.

You may like to say now:
"In the name of All Love and All Truth, I now fully accept responsibility for my heart's ability to reveal to me its secrets for my complete physical, emotional, mental and spiritual health. I ask that this be taking place now, in the name of love and light, and in the name of my absolute divine truth."

"Heart I love you."

"Heart I love you."

"Heart I love you."

You are stepping into a space now of remembering a lost part of yourself, as you challenge your heart to bring you its power and light. You are now witnessing this aspect of yourself now just resurrecting itself. The sense of perfect resurrection brings you home to your earth. Your heart cannot whisper its secrets to you, when you are not open to the power of your earth to heal your heart. The heart can only whisper its secrets when it is earthed.

Earth your immortal heart. Go to the heart of the earth, where the truth lays dormant in your heart, waiting to reveal itself to you. You are now kissing the holy ground of Mother Earth. As you honor the Earth daily, you are feeding your heart with nourishment. Feeding your heart with nourishment brings it all you ever need to create a space of absoluteness for all there is, and will be. All there is and will be, can only manifest with a truth-filled heart.

The essence of this manifestation can only come about through a truth-filled heart. Breathe into your heart now the truth from Mother Earth.

Earth is truth. All is truth-filled on Earth. Mother Earth is totally truth-filled. She destroys, she creates, and she is cyclical. When your heart resonates to Mother Earth's heart as a truth-seeking experience you are witnessing your heart's chambers actually opening. You must just allow this process to take place gently. You must just allow your process of unfoldment to gradually grow in your life.

Let's recap this exercise for you:
Kiss Mother Earth's holy ground energetically or physically. You can gift her with a flower, shell or incense. Your heart is being fed with nourishment. Mother Earth is truthful. Your heart cannot trust unless it knows its secrets are protected. Your heart then begins its unfoldment.

If you want someone (i.e. friend, partner, etc.) to share the secrets of their heart with you, what do you do? They must trust you. How can they do this, if you are not truthful yourself to your own heart whispering its secrets to you? Allow, allow, allow.

Receiving the message of your heart's secrets brings you now the special remembering of why you came to Earth. You are witnessing the observance of all opportunities to receive this information now. Receiving information about why you have come to Earth is essential for your soul's development right now.

Each human being has a unique reason to come to Earth, take a body and receive the light of spirit made manifest. It is very important to try and imagine why "you" would take life in human form and not want to know why you landed here. It is like being a space explorer; landing on a planet or star, and not knowing why you took a body to this place. Try and re-create this picture in visualization:

I know why I am coming. I have a mission to fulfil here. What is my mission? What are my instructions in managing this assignment for the number of years I am going to be on this planet? Who is going to assist you? Your parents are an obvious choice.

For this answer; however, their own karmas often prevent them from being able to assist you.

With each human, they must find their own answer.

Free from parents, society and cultural expectation (i.e. religious, etc.). How do you do this?

Your heart's chakras (there are seven) have the answers to this mystery. For when you view life from a heart-centered perspective, The Serpent of Light within the heart awakens.

What is The Serpent of Light?

The Serpent of Light is a cosmic force of power, which pierces through the illusion of being human. You may not quite understand how the heart could have seven chakras (energy belts) however, it does, and when they are awakened, you begin to summon the serpent to activate. The serpent is a symbol in all cultures of power and mastery over darkness and evil.

Right now visualizing your serpent in the heart center activating and energizing yourself, the nurturing center at the base of your heart. If you imaginatively draw your own heart, you can visualize The Serpent of Light activating your self-nurturing center at the base chakra of your heart. Each portal within the heart has a god/goddess assigned to it. The ancient Egyptians believed this. (Refer to The

Carmel Glenane

Book of The Dead – Spell 125 page 129 (Allen 1974) These portals are chakras. Passing through the portal/chakra opens up the pattern of fear; which is your inner enemy needing to be conquered.

Allowing the need to be heard by a god/goddess in Ancient Egypt, (as well as being protected) ensured your own fears (demons) were challenged. Fighting your own enemy (your fears) is often the very reason for preventing you from taking the first step into self-mastery.

If you see a representation of your heart as being a living template for your own light temple, you will begin to get the enormity of what you are capable of achieving in your Earth life. You must just allow your own power of allowing your heart to respond to this new view of your totality brings you all you need to receive the light of your fully illuminated heart.

Right now just pause; allow yourself this breath; this enormity to percolate your consciousness. Visualize The Great Pyramid of Giza or Chichen Itza in Mexico to be the living template for your consciousness, resting firmly in your heart.

Pick up your heart, feel it as a pulsing, living organ, alive and powerful. Really try to imagine its secrets, its power.

Now feel it going into The Pyramid, being part of the enormity of the consciousness of the hearts of all who knew the secrets of the heart, and created these structures symbolically as living reminders of our hearts' truth. Our hearts live in these star gates. These star gates are portals for your heart to become awakened as a living pyramid. Suddenly the landscape changes. Your reality becomes heart centered. This is your pyramid. It is now inside you. Feel the energy and consciousness give you power, concentration and light.

When you ask with your clear intention from your heart's truth; the Mayan teachings reveal you will manifest through The Father (Itzamna, sacred knowledge), The Mother (Ixcheel, Mother Nature, the Earth), The Son (Kukuulkaan, the Christ, love, sun). These teaching parallel with the Egyptian teachings of The Father (Osiris), The Mother (Isis) and The Son (Horus).

The Miracle of Mysteries Revealed through the Hearts Secrets

Allowing yourself to really understand what your heart's intentions are bring to you these powers. Try and imagine now these ancient wonders of creation through these sacred cosmologies combine with their intent matching your intent, bringing you all you need to receive love. For what is love if it cannot be expressed through your heart's truth? It is only an illusion, bringing fear, chaos and non-integration.

It is now time to visualize your pyramid again with these complied sacred forces being made ready for you to receive.

"*I now bring balanced heart-centered love to me now.*"

Write this statement on your pyramid (your heart's template) evoking the forces of The Father, The Mother and The Son.

(Some religious systems also have a similar cosmology.)

This sacred secret heart begins now to burst open to the power of these divinities made manifest for you allowing you your own heart's truth express itself through all aspects of your totality, your divinity, your truth.

"*This is your birth right after all. This is why you took a body; to manifest your divinity in human form.*"

Seeing through the eyes of your heart brings spirit into resonance with your truth. Your truth, your heart is revealed in your eyes. When you witness the vision of seeing with spirit eyes, second sight, you are witnessing your heart's eyes open. Your heart's visionary capabilities open when you acknowledge to yourself that you are able to do this.

"*I am capable of allowing my heart's eyes to open. My heart's eyes open to my truth. Truth and I are one, in the manifestation of my vision through my heart's eyes.*"

You are allowing now your visionary capacity to create with your heart's eyes, your truth. In Ancient Mayan teachings the circle represents the feminine aspect of creation, and the black dot, the masculine aspect of creation. This is called Hunab Kuk, (our own eyes, right masculine, left feminine.) Our feminine and masculine selves are balanced in our eyes. Our heart's eyes are the barometers for this emerging truth, and witnessing it opens up your view of humanity, your heart's humanity unbelievably.

In The Book of The Dead (Allen 1974) – Spell 112 page 91: Horus's adversary Seth in Egyptian cosmology states:

"Behold my eye (feels) as (it did at) that blow with Seth, struck at my eye."

Ra states, to the gods, as Horus's eye was gouged out in a bloody battle with Seth. Horus was to be given Imset, Hapi, Duamutef and Qubehsenuf to protect his sacred truth, which comes through Horus's eyes.

(These beings correspond to the Eastern, Southern, Western and Northern Quarters.)

What is being expressed here is a powerful and sacred truth:
Accept the responsibility of what your heart's eyes are seeing, and protect what you are witnessing and share with others.

To receive the illuminated truth of your heart's secrets, you are witnessing much grief and loss in your total being. You must surrender this little self, who thinks she knows love. This little self is a servant, not a master. As a servant, she observes, listens and obeys the instructions of the master (the heart), who reveals its secrets. She (the little self) must be respectful in the face of what her own intelligent heart is capable of. She must learn and grow. Furthermore she must be encouraged to grow in a human body, which houses the universe's secrets. What a responsibility you, "The Master" who has to train and instruct your "emotional heart" to listen to and obey "The Master," the intelligent heart.

She cannot know the truth because "her" consciousness hasn't witnessed the expansion and growth of all she is capable of. Right now, allowing "you," your fully opened intelligent heart to be your totality is the greatest challenge, because the child, the servant, wants to have her own needs met at the expense of the total picture, the grand plan of your heart's secrets.

What a gift you are giving yourself right now.

"Am I able to give myself this gift?"

"How am I going to manage the child, the servant?"

You must allow yourself to surrender your need to manage this wayward aspect of yourself. Feel this now, feel the mergence, which comes with the surrender to merge with your totally new, fully awakened, secret intelligent heart.

"I now lovingly surrender to the full remembering of my heart's secrets, and I allow myself to observe my wayward servant, my emotional heart, from ever interfering with my truth, my totality now."

Believing that you, the owner (or managing director of your heart), gives you an unbelievable sense of raw power and courage to begin this task.

Ask yourself:
"Am I going to listen to my intelligent heart that has access to universal wisdom, truth and knowledge? Or

Am I going to continue to be the victim of my needy child self, who hooks into every emotion, every thought of her wandering mind and emotional heart?"

You are now allowing the energy of this new secret self bring you the power of all you ever were and will be. The greatest level of protection a heart can have is in the moment of witnessing your own emotional self and not giving it energy. It is only fear that gives your enemy (your emotional self out of control) its power.

This is now a time to recognize the enormity of protection, to enable The Master, the awakened luminous heart, to deliver its secrets to the remaining parts of your intelligences of which are under the guardianship of the fully awakened heart.

As described in the teachings of the Mayans, the two-headed serpent, The Serpent of Light, the sacred knowledge brings All Love, strength, wisdom, power and truth. It integrates the sky and moon. The sacred mythology of Ancient Egypt also saw the two-headed serpent as a symbol of mastery and integration. Not only physically, but also a sense of unity of upper and lower Egypt; hence all pharaohs who were under the guardianship of their gods and goddesses, who too wore crowns with double-headed serpents.

Imagine yourself now being a two-headed serpent, like the Maya who saw themselves as children of cosmic wisdom. You can create this through the activation of your heart's two-headed serpent. Ask for this activation to take place now. This activation brings you now into resonance with all there is. This is a time to really acknowledge to yourself your worthiness to receive this wisdom from our ancient ancestors.

Right now attune to the serpents of the Earth, which hold the secrets for Earth's evolving humanity. Feel the energy of the serpent uncoiling from the great heart of Mother Earth herself. As the serpent courses its way through the Earth's energy belts and chakras, feel it arriving in your own heart chakra, your "self" center. Your serpent self awakens. Your heart's serpent begins its ascent by merging with the fire serpent of the Earth.

As the energy opens through your heart center, you will begin to feel it, hear it, taste it, smell it and see the serpent merging with your heart serpent, as the serpent begins its uncoiling. It is now uncoiling through your heart, where it becomes the one serpent with two heads.

The feeling of the serpent growing two heads may take some time for you to connect to. It doesn't matter, just remember to grow two heads, you are just beginning the integratory process.

The integratory process takes place through the Earth itself, who summons the serpent of the Earth to bring you this mergence, and oneness with all your energy selves, and begin the integratory process. As the mind begins to separate itself, the energy of All Love can become part of your totality.

This process is one of extreme caution. So powerful is it that it can create a great energy "explosion" in the heart. Respect for such a process is needed. Ask your fully awakened intelligent heart to guide you in this process, and always check in with Mother Earth whose home in fire serpent lives in.

You are exploring a deeply held belief in your heart's ability to heal every single aspect of your cellular remembering. This activation can bring up suppressed grief. Activations of the heart's cellular remembering allows you to resonate to the power of the heart cellular remembering. When the heart remembers, it is communicating with you the power of your Akashic records, which are stored primarily in your cells. Accessing the Akashic records is an acknowledgment that you, your totality is being honored and listened to.

Following the path of your heart's intelligence is allowing you through cellular remembering to become one with All Love, All Truth and the "All." The "All" of anything that loves becomes "one" with your "All." Translating this information into human consciousness allows you to become one with "All." The "All" of every living thing.

Flow in this energy, focus and be aware of the power, light and truth your remembering allows. All = All. All to become one with your totality. You allow the "All." You allow the mergence of your beingness to resonate with your totality.

For humans, the serpent links the power of cosmic remembering of the "All." The serpent in all cultures is then in fact the "All," the totality of beginning and ending. Our serpent mythology is as old as time itself, being called, "The umbilical cord of the new born" and "evolving Earth."

As Horus the Divine falcon god of Ancient Egypt was given Divine Kingship; it is stated in "The Book of the Dead" (Allen 1974):

"his Cobra headdress is 'The Whole Land'; even the Black Land and the Red Land of Ancient Egypt are described as being at peace as they toil for thy "Cobra Headdress."

Imagine yourself as Horus, The Divine King, wearing your "Cobra Headdress" now.

Allowing this consciousness to percolate through your cellular remembering creates in you a sense of awe for the power being you are. The energy of it must be integrated slowly and lovingly for yourself now, as you begin to uncoil like the serpent.

You are slowly remembering from your winter hibernation of slumber in remembering your humanness and its enormous potential. You are allowing now the power of all you ever were begin the remembering process now, as you shake off all your winter coverings. This cellular remembering acknowledges the heart of every living cell, as you go back to your time of being "a cell."

When you see yourself as a cell with a heart forming, you are beginning to chart a new direction for your life as a human embryo. As our cells multiply and divide; the cellular remembering becomes lost in the division of the cells. Right now you can awaken and take yourself back to this first cell.

I am a cell. At a point I begin to remember is when I begin to evolve. For it is when we begin to remember "who" we really are, is when we begin to recognize our potential.

Our remembering has encoded in it all we ever were and will be, and begins with one tiny cell; you as a cell. For now witnessing your perfect completed cell with full remembering. At this moment this fusion with your remembering brings you all you need to receive. The energy of receiving has encoded in it this remembering, for when you remember is when you receive.

Cellular remembering is just that. It is the activation of the first cell in its remembered state. Go into yourself, as a cell, by visualizing yourself as a balloon (make it iridescent). You are floating in it as consciousness. Your consciousness now is fully alive to your potential in it remembering. The first remembering is sound, which comes through vibration.

What is the sound you are hearing in this remembered state?

This sound is the sound of remembering for you. It is the place where you had your first remembering experience. This place of remembering is being encoded through your cell now.

Feel now your cell multiplying and talking to the other cells; recoding them to remember the first sound. This process brings with it much power, as your body begins to awaken to the "Sound of Remembering."

What is the "Sound of Remembering?"

Going through this process with all your senses open (i.e. seeing, hearing, tasting, touching and smelling) begins the journey into the most secret part of yourself, the secret part of your remembering. To remember is not to forget who you really are. I remember who I really am. When this process begins to activate in you, you are finding your heart open and respond to its complete unlimited potential. This process may take some time.

You may ask: *What will happen in my life when remembering my heart's secrets takes place?*

Firstly you will not feel fear in the "ordinary" way: There will be an acknowledgement of the fear; however, the usual defence mechanisms for fear close down, and you can see yourself in your absolute totality. When the usual mechanisms that govern our lives (which are fear based) are gone, we are free to create in human bodies all that our hearts came here to experience.

Our hearts came to Earth to experience the embodiment of All Love and All Truth in all intelligences fully operating and totally functioning as one "whole," not dis-embodied parts.

You can offer your cell, your first remembering, to the great mother, Mother Earth. Imagine now Mother Earth taking your cell and blessing/consecrating it, telling it you are safe to begin the journey in a body with all your remembering intact.

To honor the process of remembering is to acknowledge a force, a mighty power you have, but choose not at some level to access. Why would you choose not to access the help of a dignitary that you have an intimate connection with? Imagine now accessing the power of yourself as this dignitary; this powerful, wise, abundant, trusting being. This being is yourself, and it is yourself in your first remembering whom you must pay homage to every day, or hourly if in need.

Allow yourself to remember now the last time you felt completely fearful, anxious, etc. Feel the picture of yourself at that time of great fear. Visualize yourself calling that being.

Begin your dialogue; it may go like this:
"Help me please, use all your contacts to help me. I am in trouble. I can't see my way through this. Help me please."

The most challenging part is to say to yourself that the dignitary can help you. We would happily believe that our "friend" will assist in our totally fearful state. This dignitary is your remembered "self," your heart's remembering. It is hard for us in our non-remembered state to conceive of such an intelligence that has so many contacts to help us in our hour of need.

Every part of us has this remembrance encoded in us, every organ, even our viscera and bones. Let's begin a journey to this remembered self.

Greet Mother Earth, she has consecrated your first cell, remember? Now put the cells to work. Let's get them doing some remembering for us:

Bring the remembering firstly into your heart. Heart you are being entrained to remember me as a god or goddess or a most empowered multidimensional being you could think of. Your heart will begin the search for the "remembering," by being told it has the remembering encoded in it. When this activation begins to take place you can feel yourself renewing yourself with energy. Honor yourself totally, completely. Begin with your hair, brain, eyes, every organ, skin, bones and marrow, right to the thighs, calves and toes.

> ** Eyes; you have the power of remembering; see clearly for me now, my truth.*
>
> ** Ears; you have the power of remembering; hear clearly for me now, my truth.*
>
> ** Every organ, every single part of you can be regularly entrained for this remembering.*

This portion of ourselves can be made as an offering to our fully awakened intelligent hearts. The heart is the seat of intelligence, the source of all power. The essence of remembered self will begin with entraining the heart's intelligence. It has the master switch for all aspects of the remembered self.

You are witnessing this source remembering take place right now in your core central matrix. This remembering is now encoding you to really allow the preciousness of all you ever were bring you the power of this remembered self. Allowing this remembering now brings you into the space of truth for the remembering itself. The remembering itself is the sum total of all you ever were and will be. This is a journey, a sense of true understanding of the remembered state.

Loving the experience of the remembering, loving the experience of all there is in the remembered state brings you a sense of unimaginable peace and light. Flow in the essence of this remembering now, as you allow the source energy of remembering to come to you.

You are allowing this remembering bring you all you need now to awaken to the power of the heart's capacity to remember its power.

Right now the balance of remembering brings you to the seat of your own power to resist your own need to fight your own enemy. Your enemy is your remembering. In your enemy, your remembering, you are remembering the "enemy of remembering" which is your own fear of facing your "enemy of remembering." This enemy is yourself. You are quite simply your own enemy. The enemy is yourself and it is sharing you with the knowledge of remembering. You are just fearful of the very thing you are. This is your own enemy. Your remembering can strike you, because you are facing the challenge of saying to yourself you must abandon your old way of being, of allowing this old self to have any control over you at all; so your enemy is your remembering. Your subconscious, which stems from its reptilian survival, will strike you against the very thing you want; your remembered self.

Be ruthless with your own resistance here; be totally ruthless. Feeling yourself deep in the tomb of your remembered self, facing the enemy of yourself against the true beauty and power of your gleaming heart, a true portal of remembering. You are slithering around in the underworld if you do not strike out against your own silent killer against the heart's truth, its love and intelligence to create a magical miraculous life for you.

Right now the essence of this remembering is being encoded on you for the absoluteness in the remembering right now. Feel the power, the essence and mighty intelligence of your heart speak to you, through this enemy of remembering—yourself. Now.

The energy of remembering your heart's truth brings you the power to create in your world the essence of all you ever were. Your heart is a portal to infinity: It is the only organ in your body which is a portal, and you are recognizing your power to create with it as a portal.

This is time to really resurrect your heart's remembering as a portal and allow yourself this "remembering." Right now you are witnessing your extraordinary capacity to see the heart for what it is; a portal of remembering. You are allowing this power to bring you all you need right now to trust in the forces of remembering. Allowing the forces of remembering to create with you brings you to a state of acceptance of all there is. This state of acceptance of all there is, allows the energy of all life to create with you. All of life is a creative energizing process. You are witnessing your own river of life widen into the portal of the ocean and the primordial depth of the seas and the underworld.

This is a time of this remembering; when this remembering is activated all of life becomes a portal of power and light. You are witnessing your own capacity to really tap into this source now, as the essence of all life begins to create with you in the magic of all there ever was.

Right now allow the power, energy and light to bring you to the power, essence and life force of this remembered state. This remembered state of all you ever were; all now your magician's power, which is your heart's secret remembering, bring you all you need to receive the most precious and magical gift, the gift of remembering your power to know you have the most incredible power resting in your chest.

You are imagining right now in your consciousness a world where the heart is the central apex in all of creation. Your creative journey in life must sign post you to the heart. Every act leads to the heart. For the heart, once opened, has an enormous capacity to flow energy in and out, like a lotus flower, opening and receiving more light and energy. Recognition of this portal of remembering brings you all you need to receive the light of power and illumination.

You are allowing the power of illumination to create with you in all aspects of your remembering now as the preciousness of all you ever were brings you this sense of knowing now. Arriving at this portal is like a huge bonfire lighting up the night sky. You are aware of this opening now, as you meditate on your heart's bonfire lighting up the night sky. The essence of your own power to create this template in your remembering brings you the knowledge that you can really create in the mystery of all there is.

Allowing this brings you to the space of absolute trust that absolutely every living thing in the universe and beyond is interconnected and hangs by this mystical thread.

You are allowing the essence of this mystic thread to bring you a sense of pure bliss and acceptance of all there ever was and will be. This sense of preciousness, of absoluteness, binds all of creation together.

All of creation is bound by this thread of this precious knowing that the heart once opened connects to this invisible thread. The source of creativity itself.

The essence of your heart's remembering comes from the power of knowing that the heart of The Mysteries is the knowledge that it is The Mother that gives permission for the Akasha to be opened, so the truth of your heart's knowing can be revealed to you. An ancient Mayan teaching reveals that only The Mother can give "The Lord" permission to open the Akashic records.

The Akashic records are storehouses of ancient information about your heart's blue print in its many incarnations and cycles. This knowledge brings you a secret power; to evoke "The Mother" first. You will be able to help yourself find your way through the labyrinth of lifetimes your soul was exposed to in the cycle repeating the same pattern over and over again in its many incarnations on Earth and elsewhere. Finding a space, an empty space within yourself to access this wisdom of your soul remembering is part of why you created this incarnation for yourself in the first place.

The ancient Mayans tell us that to access the wisdom of our own heart's remembering through the Akashic records brings us to a point of remembering to evoke The Mother to give permission to The Lord to give the sacred information to you; the wandering lost child. You are witnessing this principle in accessing this long-forgotten information when you ask why you are denied information about an aspect of your suffering self, so she can heal. Give yourself permission to access this forbidden forgotten, information through the masculine (Lord) and the forgotten feminine (Mother).

To begin to feel the heart as a construction of a reality you wish to create, brings you into alliance with the purpose behind the construction itself.

Ask yourself: *What do I want to construct in my life?*

It may be mundane or spiritual. A mundane quest only constructs with the emotional heart. It cannot construct with a greater or finer material, because the emotional body is not able to re-create itself. For example, you can construct a house of paper or straw; how long will it last? Now imagine you are constructing a house from the finest materials available; that can withstand time itself. You are able to witness yourself in this construction of your heart now. Using the heart as a building material of the finest imaginable crystal, you are building your heart for its immortality. To allow yourself to create a world built on desire, illusion and need only sees the template of the heart's remembering being torn to shreds. You must decide. Your heart has its challenge in overcoming its emotional needs for love, pleasure, happiness, etc. against The Higher Truth of its calling.

What is this heart's calling?
The calling of the heart to construct its immortality through being in a human body only reinforces its power to master the emotional limitations of its construction: You are witnessing the alchemical process of the heart's remembering begin to take control over how it wants to be constructed for its journey in a human body. I must sift through the emotional debris, human mundane life, this incarnation imposes on it. Its sole task is to witness the emotional body controlling the choice of building materials and keep asking: *"Is this the only material available for my immortal heart in this human incarnation?"*

Ask yourself daily:
"What am I constructing today?"

"Is the material I am giving myself good enough?"

"Is there a better or finer material for me to construct my Heart's Temple to have an immortal life?"

When you constantly reject what your emotions and mind present you with; and can constantly and consistently look for a "higher grade construction material," you are able to say to yourself; *"Is this really good enough for what I am constructing right now?* My heart wants more than this." You must challenge always the first reaction you are presented with and go beyond it.

"Is this person good enough for my immortal heart?"

"Is this job, career, home good enough for me to build my immortal heart from the finest materials?"

Keep challenging continually what you are being presented with. Always ask: *"Is this relationship, these people around me, this environment, good enough; is there something better?"*

Your remembered heart will tell you. Call it home, start constructing your heart's temple from the finest and best material available.

You are allowing now your heart to be part of your totality by connecting to your own heart and protecting it, so your soul (higher self) can continue the journey with you. This is time to really contain the vibration, which attaches to the soul while completing its incarnation in a human incarnation.

For the soul/higher self and heart must always be made one. They are wandering, lost, not connected to the source, the power station of their totality. This disconnection has at its heart the essence, energy and life force, which is essential in the human journey and in the afterlife.

The energy you put into connecting your heart with its source of power; through the soul and the higher self sees you investing in the greatest thing imaginable; you are investing in your totality. This totality has at its center, the central core matrix of your beginning. The central core matrix of your beginning has at its essence the belief that you are always abundantly connected to the source of all life and the source of your power to receive love. Your totality is dependent upon this unification. In "The Book of the Dead" (Allen 1974) the ancient Egyptians composed very elaborate spells for this unification. As a philosophy, their belief was this unification, which the ultimate purification created. The ultimate and total integration of all selves was and is the most powerful reminder for why we are here and have taken a body. Keeping the connection alive and clear is the most important ingredient for the soul's peace.

To begin the journey into your own underworld/afterlife creates in you the total belief that you have many "selves" to integrate. These energy bodies have their own frequency and vibration and can be attuned to systematically.

Imagine yourself now having all these energy bodies/subtle selves and your primary task in being human is to integrate them, i.e. getting them activated and working harmoniously together. You are allowing your own heart to spread its wings, to open it more and more to attune to these different frequencies/vibrations that vibrate to your own consciousness in acknowledging them. These "selves" become portals and when activated can "talk" to each other, and support your totality in a human body. The subtlety, yet intensity of light coming from these energy fields when activated create a very powerful vortex of light. These portals can be activated, and when properly working are like fairy lights in all different colors, holding different levels of consciousness for you to experience. This luminosity brings with it a rush of power and energy.

Imagine now all these portals activating, opening and revealing the subtlety of your totality back to you. You are merging in this awareness now. To go into this activation requires "you" to really feel outside the density of one of your bodies, the physical to encompass all the subtle bodies.

The Five Bodies: The ancient traditions teach us that there are five bodies.

They are: *The Spiritual Body; The Magical Body (which is less subtle); The Shadow Body; The Double Body and The Physical Body.*

Ancient Egyptian Mystery Schools called them: *The SaHu; The Kfu; The Haidit; The Ka; and The Aufu.*

Under the direction of the awakened heart's intelligence, you can activate these subtle bodies. When the heart's intelligence is awakened, the subtle bodies become activated as well. This process is subtle, yet powerful and can be done in ritual meditation, by awakening your heart's intelligences for integration and mergence.

These energies are subtle yet powerful. They are performed ideally at certain times, i.e. certain phases of the moon, when the heart is most receptive. As an endocrine gland, the heart responds to the moon phases. Your heart tells you when you are able to integrate these powerful, yet often destructive, energies.

In the book "The Goddess Sekhmet" (Masters R 2010) he discusses the ancient Egyptian Mystery School teachings through The Goddess Sekhmet. "The Way of The Five Bodies" Mystery school, instructed that they had to be opened at different levels, not sequentially. Allowing these bodies within you to be under the direction of you own higher self is the safest way. As we evolve, we must respect that those in our lives (partners, family, lovers, etc.) may not want the level of evolvement that you may want with this person. Hearts can be cleared for evolvement, however free will is respected. Performing the tantric rituals between couples must have full consent of surrender of both people.

When we begin to contemplate the enormity of the responsibility to live with this truth in our heart we begin to realize how our hearts create with us intelligently. For this truth to manifest brings a sense of almighty strength and power to our whole being. You are witnessing this power to create with these energy selves every moment you intone your heart's truth to receive this power. You are allowing this almighty power to bring you the responsibility to only live with this single belief. You are now bringing this power into your own being, when you create in the essence of your heart's ability to regenerate itself through these activations.

You create in this energy by allowing the frequency of your heart to actually talk to all your energy selves, and in truth getting them to activate each other. As one opens it can send its intelligence directly to other energy selves. Each subtle body becomes activated and infused with its own innate capacity to really create with you.

Feeling this ability to create with you allows your own power to manifest for you. The energy of all these manifested selves cannot be equated in your definition of your own reality.

The essence of allowing you the belief in five primary intelligences working in full communication with you can be entrained upon you now. Imagine now being the commander; this energy is like having an army of soldiers who at your instruction open your senses to receive all you need for your life right now.

The power and enormity of activating the heart's energy portals is a transformational experience, allowing you now to really tap into the source of all you ever were in your remembering.

The essence of this allowing must be entrained upon your cellular memory first, as your cellular memory will begin to allow these activations to manifest. The cellular memory once awakened begins to burst with information about your cellular truth. All cells have encoded in them truth for remembering. You are allowing your own heart its journey in this cellular remembering now. Flow in this essence, and really allow your own heart its magical truth. Flow in the essence of this remembering now.

You can send healing to your own energy selves by asking for your intelligent heart, to create a magnetic force around you whole being, i.e. your energy field, light body and aura and create in this activation your remembering.

You may intone:
"In the name of 'All Love and All Truth,' I now co-create with my heart's intelligence the fully awakened intelligence of all I ever was and will be.

I am asking that all my energy selves at the five levels of remembering bring me into resonance with my truth and light."

You are activating these energy portals to live with full embodiment of your heart's intelligence. You are flowing in this energy and light now. This is a most powerful and sacred time in your remembering.

Visualize now these energetic selves being activated under the heart's direction. Your intelligent heart knows what is needed at this level of your consciousness. The heart knows the secrets of its own truth, and your heart is your very best friend, one who cannot betray you. Make a pact with your own heart to be very best friends. You may like to lovingly intone to your heart to be fully engaged in your journey to its bliss and full integration in a human body. By living in your own luminous light body, you become a beacon of light for your remembering. This is time to activate this remembering with your bliss-filled heart. Living with a bliss- filled heart feeds light into your whole being. This beingness creates in this energy all you ever were and will be.

Living in the heart's intelligence births the opportunity to grow in a way you cannot yet imagine. The heart of your amazing new world will respond to the energy downloads you receive, and you begin to live and feel in a way not previously thought possible. When you awaken to this energy, you will be alighting your own luminous light body; living completely in it.

Your "netherworld" is your fear. When you cross out your fear, you are reborn to be joy-filled every moment. Flowing in this golden light of your triumphant newly resurrected self pours light and power into your fear. You are free of this fear. You are free to bring to your world your power to find this light in your heart and light up your whole universe.

This is time to really find your own relationship with your heart bring you all you need to receive the message your heart brings you. You are alchemizing in the energy of this remembered state now as you birth your new template to truth. You are opening up your relationship with all there is as this alchemizing takes place. Allowing the alchemizing to create with you now brings you into resonance with all there is. You have released to this aspect of yourself, as you bring to your world your power and light to receive love.

Accessing this wisdom, living in the energy of it, brings you peace and light. You are opening up your own pathway to remembering your power in a way not thought possible previously. You are flooding your cellular memory with this power and light as you access this portal of remembering.

Flowing in the special remembering brings you all you need to really allow yourself this peace and light. You are accessing this power and light now, and it is this part of you, you must attune to, to receive all you need now. You are in a space of remembering, continuously you intone:
"I am now accessing my fully remembered self."

"I am free to remember."

"I am safe in remembering."

"Remembering brings me power."

Feeling the power of remembering allows you now to really respond to a part of yourself that knows this truth and lives it. You are allowing now your own special belief in all you were to bring you all you ever need to receive magical remembering for your fully awakened heart.

Now you are really ready to begin to see with the eyes of your heart, and flow in this energy of power and light. You are enveloping yourself now in your own heart's mystery, which brings power to your very being.

You are opening the way; evoking your own heart's mystery to create with you. When you flow in this mystery, you are addressing your belief in surrendering to the forces assisting you right now.

Feel now your heart on the starry boat of heavens, offering yourself as a channel for your own resurrection. You are opening and reflecting on this mystery, as the new happenings start to explode in your consciousness. Right now see yourself sitting on the boat of heavens, flowing in the starry magnificence of your heart's remembering. Watch as the day opens to you, sailing high, flowing in the masculine majesty of the noon-day sun, releasing to the softness of the evening sunset, as your boat glides, now through the portals of the underworld, only to be born again. Feel now your heart being part of the magnificence of its own creation.

As you are flowing now on the newly resurrected aspect of yourself you witness your birth, you are remembering to really create in this magnificence; your world brings to you the glory of this power of your heart's creation. Your heart creates every day to remember. It creates in this remembering all it ever was and will be. Flow in this boat. Feel the power of your heart's remembering in this energy now.

Creating in the energy of this heart's power brings to you the absolute essence of your divinity in human form. This is time to really flow in the energy of all your selves as you begin the cycle of renewal. Feel yourself now in this world of true trust for all there is. You are allowing your own sense of majesty and power to bring you all you need to create in the world of absoluteness for all there is.

Flow now in the rainbow magnificence of all you ever were as you allow now the magic of all your selves bring themselves into harmony with all of life. You are allowing this sense now the power of your heart's truth bring all you need to love. You are allowing now the energy of completeness to bring you all you need now to create in a world of true trust for the mystery.

Creating in this magic, this essence brings you to the point of total surrender for all there is. You are flowing now in this absoluteness as you dissolve into your power. The heart of All Love is your truth now as you begin to really accept the responsibility for creating in this world a model for all of life. You are answering the call to awaken to your power to remember now, all you ever were and will be. Just flow in the newly remembered power now. Flow in the light of your newly remembered power.

You are witnessing in your beingness now the totality of all your selves, and all you are capable of right now. This is your time to really say:
"I am flowing in the power of my newly created heart. I am allowing this power to resurrect me."

Right now the allowance for the heart to create through you must be observed continually against the enemy of the mind's power. You must accept and surrender to the heart's view of your reality now. Your witnessing of your mind against the heart brings a sense of peace and harmony to all your selves.

Your challenge now in observing your mind must be to see it as not anything but old stuck memory patterns, which must be observed. These are just like old recordings, which keep playing their same tune. This is time to really allow the essence of all you ever were to create with you, and allow the preciousness of all you ever were to create with you.

Flowing in this energy brings you a sense of observance of your mind's constant need to dominate the unfolding of your heart's truth. Observing the heart like a sacred blue lotus unfolding on a perfectly still lily pond brings you to the point of absoluteness for the mystery of your heart's unfoldment, against your mind's need to challenge the growth with its power.

This is the challenge in your evolvement now.

"Am I able to witness my mind against my heart's truth?"

Am I able to say "Yes" I can be a guard against my mind's need to dominate my process of enfoldment right now?"

I feel this challenge every moment. My mind will create a barrier; however, it is only a moment. This challenge will present itself; know it will be there and protect your own heart's truth against it. Protect the blue lotus of your heart's immortality, as you are now immersing yourself in a world of pure light as you take your heart to the bathing pool of pure light offering it as a gift to the almighty hearts of light, peace and order.

You are ritualistically saying to yourself:
"I am offering my heart as a ritual instrument in service to the great ones."

The feeling must be one of reverence for this anointing, as you bring to your world the sense of wonder for what your heart is capable of. Allowing this precious gift of your heart's intelligence be one of absoluteness for its own creation right now. Allowing this to flood the heart with light, power and order brings to you the sacredness of life as a co-creative tool. Acknowledging your heart as a co-creative tool brings to you the power and light of all your senses working in unison with each other. The endocrine/hormonal function becomes stronger, able to create with you. You are witnessing this metamorphosis in consciousness right now.

Allowing this absoluteness, this power to see yourself in absoluteness brings to you the magic and light of all you ever were: You are allowing your own offering, your own heart's offering to bring you all you need to create a world of real truth and magic for all there is.

The space you give yourself gives your heart its honor as a sacred vessel of light, a light beacon, able to guide you through the challenges presented to you every day. This is time to trust the mighty power of your heart, it has been consecrated and honored in its capacity to help you in this dimension. Allow now the principle of all you ever were to be in reverence with your heart's capacity to really create with you all you need to remember truth.

The acceptance of your own heart's truth in allowing this remembering brings you to a space of truth and ownership of all you ever were. You are flowing in the knowledge that you are able to really allow your heart to bring you the power of its almighty truth.

The Miracle of Mysteries Revealed through the Hearts Secrets

This is a flowing and mergence in the forces of oneness for all there is, as you take your remembering back to its source. Right now you are allowing the energy of this power of your heart's earth, its truth to become one with you. Allowing this energy brings even more power, truth and light to your core being. This core being takes you into this heart, this remembering now, as the essence of all you ever were creates with you in the mystery.

The mystery of the creation is in you now, as you bring your almighty power into resonance with your truth. You are allowing this source, this remembering to bring you to your heart. Your heart is in the oneness of all and "All" creates with you. You are vibrating to this "All" as the heart awakens to its pure power and truth to create with you.

Respecting your heart, respecting its source remembering allows you to really come to the essence of the experience of beingness. The experience of beingness floods your immortal heart with its truth. Flow in the river of pure magical firepower now as you awaken to the mystery of all you ever were. Allow the essence of this mystery, create in wonder for all. The all brings the absolute totality of allowance now for you to receive. Flow in the energy of this allowing, this mergence, this remembering now.

Your heart now begins to create with the almighty power of remembering, as you awaken from your humanness. You won't be able to identify with the human condition as much. You will begin to see yourself as an earthling. You are a heart, living as an earthling for a period of time. Imagine a visitor staying with you, she stays for a while, she partakes in the ceremony of your world, she learns, grows and moves on to another world.

When you see yourself in this frequency, you become an earthling. You become one with the mystery, you partake in the drama of humankind, but you don't identify with it, you are in fact an earthling; just flowing in the energy of the Earth, its elements and its form. Your identification is with nature, the natural world and its forces.

You become detached from the drama of humanness, as you begin to become aware of so many different intelligences, vibrating to so many different frequencies calling you.

This is time to resonate to this call, this magical call to create a world of pure peace and light for the mystery. You are transiting to a new view of your humanity, feeling the heart of every living thing, at different frequencies. These intelligences matching your intelligence as your heart responds to a new view of life that sees you connecting — humanely instead of humanly.

To become an earthling is to see your heart, its truth, resonating with these forces, these intelligences, rather than your human condition.

Allowing the sacred forces through Mother Earth's elements, quarters, forces and intelligences allows you to partake in the drama of human life, without the emotional and mental slavery you impose on yourself. Flowing in this merging brings to you peace and light. You are living entirely through your heart consciousness, as you embrace the world of peace and light for being human. This energy has at its heart your own power to recognize yourself as an oracle of the heart.

The heart is very alive and responsive to your truth. Your truth and your heart marry in a rainbow infusion of light and power; merging in oneness for all there is. This light and mergence brings order, light and power to you right now. You are opening up to your own power, light and love in this mergence right now. You own this energy right now as you open up to all you ever were and will be. You are allowing your heart to create in this vortex of raw magical power now as your heart is remembering its power. It is alive to your acknowledgement of it. You are flowing in this energy now. You are allowing this energy to gather and bring you all you need right now to really create the world you deserve.

You are allowing now your energy to drive you deeply into your core; your central core matrix to bring peace, light and magical renewal to your world. You are allowing this peace and light to gather. Flowing in this mystical power of your being, to really say:
"*I have so much power, wisdom and light right inside my chest.*"

"*It is beating to the world of absoluteness and light.*"

"*It is beating to the call of The Mother.*"

"*I am alive to its call now.*"

You can send energetic messages to human hearts, and ask them how they are doing, how do they need support? You can share happy moments with others hearts this way in human or divine form.

Allowing the mergence into this oneness creates a force of unbelievable power, as you truly alchemize your heart's remembering. You are vibrating to the world of real truth and power, allowing the sense of all you ever were to bring you all you ever will be. This is a time for creating in this alchemizing force now, as you begin to find your own true power of remembering. The power of remembering brings with it a sense of real joy and peace for all you ever were.

You are allowing now the joy, the peace of all you ever were to bring you alive to the mystery. You are alive to the spectacle of your remembering now, as you really allow the heart of all you ever were to bring this energy and light to you. Flow in this power, this energy, this light gives you an unbelievable sense of renewal. You are feeling in the renewal the power of the forces assisting you, and you are in honor of these forces.

Being in reverence for these forces, and alchemizing them to you through the balanced heart's elements and quarters stabilizes your whole beingness. This beingness has encoded in it, you, and your totality for the mergence of all there ever was. Allowing this mergence to co-create with you now creates a vibration of true and lasting power and energy. When you witness your own ability to create in this space, you are allowing your own heart to magnetize all you ever need and will need.

You are flowing in the energy, the life force and magic of this renewal. It brings you to complete restructuring of your energy templates. These vibrations are being made available now, as your heart begins to remember all it ever was.

The wisdom of your heart's secrets encode themselves on you in many ways. You are becoming aware of how the heart will bring to you the power of all you ever were, if you just always consult with your heart when making decisions. You need to set up a signal for this to happen. Right now you are witnessing the language of your heart bring you its secrets to really magnify all you need to receive love.

You are aware of this magnification now. You are allowing the power to bring you all you need to receive the power and wisdom the heart will share with you if you set up a time with your heart every day to speak to you.

Constructing a reality of your heart as you own true oracle brings you this sense of pure safety and power to make decisions. You are witnessing your own shape-shifting in this alchemizing power of your own heart giving you your remembered truth. Your remembered truth is indeed the most powerful reminder of who you are, and will be. Feeling the heart of this remembered truth brings you all you need to witness and be part of the spectacle of your heart's remembered truth. Flow in this remembering now.

Being a channel to your remembered truth can only come through your heart. This is the absolute essence of all you ever were. This essence creates with you now in this remembering. Allow this essence to shape you now. You may like to intone:
"Heart I love you. Please share with me our remembered truth in this decision, I am needing to make about this relationship/project, etc."

You will receive the answer immediately.

The spirit of remembered truth sets the heart ablaze with fire power. The vision of observing your heart in this space reinforces your own power to shape your destiny. In allowing this spectacle of your awakened truth you are indeed witnessing a worldview of power, light and All Love.

You are allowing your essence to shine in its true enfoldment. You must feel the power of this remembered truth, and the heart's power to really create an invisible web protecting the whole energetic matrix of your totality.

The heart is a self-regulating organism. Through its extraordinary intelligence, you are witnessing the power and light of your remembering. You are allowing this remembering to challenge and dictate to your organs, the power of its force to create change in your whole physicality; i.e. the organs of the body, will respond to the heart's power. The heart has the greatest power over all the organs; however it must be given a peace-filled harmonious environment, free from anxiety and the tyrannous mind, controlling it.

The heart must be free to do its work, even in saving your life. However, for this to happen, it must be able to work it out in harmony and peace. The heart has the strength, it has the answers; however, your understanding of this principle must firstly be understood and integrated.

Allowing this sacred truth to guide you brings you to the heart of all you ever were. You are rescuing yourself from your old anxious state when you allow the heart's intelligence to guide you. The essence of your heart lives by this principle.

As you develop your own sensitivity to the power of your heart to be listened to first, and consulted for all issues in your life; you will begin to shape your own destiny. Your destiny is an organic thing, it can be shaped, and your heart is the shape-shifter. You are flowing in this mergence now. You are whispering to your heart your fears and anxieties. Tell your heart your fears, and it will respond even though you may not feel it immediately.

You are allowing this part of yourself to merge in oneness with all of life, all of life creates through the heart's intelligence all it needs to find the sense of peace and oneness for all life to be a harmonious self-regulating one. To create with this mergence, brings to you the sense of absoluteness for everything. Everything is absolute, and everything has absoluteness encoded in it. Allowing this mergence with your heart brings you a sense of sacred trust that all of life supports and protects you always.

You are allowing your own heart to bring you the sense of ownership now. You control your destiny. You sail through rough waters, storms and tempests; as you connect to your heart's intelligence, you remember it can connect with other intelligences to support it. It calls to other intelligences continually to support it when in distress from the emotional body and the mind. The anxiety can be caught before it becomes too dominant and threatens the heart's very existence.

The act of forgiveness of yourself to your heart for the enormity you place on it must too be considered in your daily practice. You are remembering now this enormous capacity of your heart's intelligence, its truth, and you must now really allow yourself to create in this space a sense of real understanding for the roles you have together. This is a time to really challenge your core, your identity by saying:

"Heart I am sorry," as you release the load you have imposed on it. It takes courage to look at your past and forgive yourself for your past.

You must allow this act of courage to envelope you now, as you allow your heart to be receptive to you, your own intelligence in recognizing its truth. You are a mighty witness to this process now. You are a co-creator in your remembering. This co-creation brings you now the raw magical power of all you ever were, as you transmit into this new reality. Your reality now creates in this essence, this remembering.

Remember what you have created. You are crafting yourself every moment you recognize the heart's intelligence to recognize its truth. It is grateful for your acknowledgement of your past self abuse to "your totality"; your evolution is shaped by this reality.

The Miracle of Mysteries Revealed through the Hearts Secrets

Your reality now creates in this essence, this remembering. Feel the heart of all you ever were in this remembering now. The heart's truth brings remembering. You are forgiving every aspect of your beingness now; this being the acknowledgment that "you" are an immortal.

Right now, you are witness to the enormity you have created; you are enacting your own power to live through your own heart's intelligence. You have had your "sorry day." I have publically announced to all my energy selves that I am sorry. The sorrow of living in a world, which doesn't know love, creates in you now raw magical power, as your serpents begin their journey home to their remembering.

Feel this now, feel your heart in its remembering. It is sobbing for joy, it has forgiven you and this enactment sees you now seized by your own power to create the world you need to receive love. Breathe that in. Allow your creation to be your guide as you envelope yourself in the joyous magical energy of all you ever were and will be.

Feeling the power of yourself magnify with your fire serpents now who fly down from the stellar realms, coursing their way down through your spinal column, drilling through you into the core of the heart, piercing the core of Mother Earth black heart, to return again back up to the base chakra into the spinal column. The ambrosia of the white serpent and the black serpent (the Djed in ancient Egypt) and (the Ku-Kull-Kahn in the Maya land Central America) pierce the illusion of the heart's pain, opening it and opening the way for the full integration of all you ever were. You are fulfilling your earthly duties now, you are honoring your heart; your earth you are free.

Feel now the power of your earth's heart create with you. This is a magical time to honor your own earth's heart. Your earth's heart keeps you protected and safe. When feeling unsafe, go down with a basket (in the basket is your heart) tell Mother Earth:
"*Protect my heart Mother Earth. I am afraid and I need help.*"

"*Human life is a frightening place for me right now. Please assist and send me healing to keep me safe.*"

"*You are my baby, my heart, and you are now keeping me safe.*"

Allow the spirit of your heart; grow in Mother Earth's rich elements, her soils, her waters, fires and her air. All her elements are in balance and they provide for you now rich, nourishing moisture to birth your intelligent heart. There can be no fear here, as Mother Earth is taking control of everything.

Fear of losing control is your enemy. Control is the enemy, and it is dominated by your own inability to see beyond your need to "have an answer." Having an answer keeps you trapped. You don't have an answer while you listen to your mind and emotional heart. You are now saying to yourself that "you" are free, you don't have to "have an answer." Having an answer limits your consciousness to third-dimensional reality. Your brain activates, through the mind needing the answer; *"No there is no answer."* There is no answer, the mind searches. You will never find the answer Mr. Mind.

You are assuming responsibility for everything that is happening in your life right now. This means that I must surrender all expectations of needing to feel in control over every area of my life. My challenge is in identifying my core deservability.

What is my core deservability?

My core deservability is to live with the daily challenge of not knowing if I have the resources to hold my heart's intelligence against the forces that can destroy it. I now commit to challenging my heart to bring me all I need to challenge the fear of me not being able to protect its growth. My heart brings me all I need, to challenge my fears of me not being able to protect its growth.

This is a breakthrough in personal consciousness. My heart *does* provide me with all I need, to bring me all I need for our evolution on Earth. You are witnessing now a new way in being human.

How am I going to manage knowing my heart has all the resources it needs for my earthly life?

You need to be gentle but firm with your heart right now.

"You have all the resources heart. My mind and emotions need training to accept this reality. How are you going to train them?"

You simply tell them.

"My intelligent heart knows the answer...and as a team, we must consult with 'her.'"

First "she" is a Feminine organ. 40% of her is MtDNA (see my book "Awaken your Immortal Intelligent Heart") (Glenane 2016) because "she" has this Feminine intelligence "she" knows the answers we don't. "She" is the "Master of the Ship." We are all the "crew." "She" is fair, but "she" needs space and harmony from us to make her decision. "Her" decision will be the fair one, and help us all live with peace and truth.

You must recognize that your whole totality, that your beingness, is dependent upon you being the master of your own ship. Sometimes when we are frightened, we don't want this responsibility. Ask yourself now:
"Do I want the responsibility of recognizing my heart is the master of the ship, and we are the crew?"

Feel now, this responsibility to yourself. Do not deceive yourself. Don't pretend that it is going to be easy. However, you must allow yourself to make a commitment with yourself to create a meaningful life with yourself. Feel that now.

You are witnessing the complete restructuring of all you ever were and will be. Your life begins to have a meaning you could never have previously imagined.

As you deepen your relationship with your heart's secret language, you begin to stop and reflect on your own path. There is a constant need to just observe the mind completely, like a 2-year-old child, ready to run wild. There is a sense of serenity in this new order you have created for yourself. This ever watchful nanny/parent never stops even for one second, always being vigilant toward the restless child's activities.

You are evolving in your own separateness from your mind and emotional heart. You begin to see your life as just separate from your "responsibility" to your "children." There is within you a constant source of your ever vigilant attention.

You become aware of how your mind will begin its day with you. You will know its patterns and its demands. Your "pre-rising" rituals can include your "Heart Speak Meditations":

"Heart I love you" for 15 minutes to establish your heart's authority over your earthly life demands. Your guard must never come down when you are on the direct path. The flow of energy to the heart brings power, guidance, courage and above all "truth." We are authentic to ourselves, and we are aware that by exposing our emotions, we are showing ourselves that we have lost authority over our totality. Witnessing a 2-year-old running wild is distressing and reflects the caregiver's lack of responsibility as a "parent" in managing the wayward child.

You are releasing right now to your core sense of identity as an individual who is not bound by anyone. Right now you are finding freedom in being totally connected to your heart's truth. This is an important breakthrough for you now, as the power of all you ever were now belongs to you. Feel that now.

Feeling the flow of your own power brings the heart into resonance with its truth you are surrendering to this new way of being every moment you witness yourself giving your power to another. You are forcing your cellular memory to accept new frequencies when you witness yourself bringing to your secret heart its message of power and truth.

Our hearts are trained to teach us, and they have laws. There is the law of the heart. Its secrets are to be obeyed. We must listen to our hearts to find these secret laws. For humans, it is very challenging to obey the laws of the heart.

The first law is: Stillness

When you are overwhelmed, just being "*still*" for 10 seconds can help save your life, when you have had a shock. To know when to be "still" gives the heart a chance to recover from the shock placed upon it. It can be heard then; when we are in shock we must try and be "still" so we can receive the information our heart wants us to receive.

Our heart is a multidimensional organism. It has multiple intelligences and you can create with these intelligences any time. Our heart has access to all the universes and beyond to bring you all you need for your day.

The second law is: Balance

Every night ask for your heart's elements to be balanced. The sacred elements of Air, Fire, Water and Earth; as your heart's elements are balancing themselves, they can create with the universal hearts; the universes, and all hearts' intelligences will at some level hear and respond to "your" heart's call. Every night before sleep, intone that your four sacred elements and quarters be balanced to create now and be specific:

"I ask tonight that my heart's sacred elements and quarters of Air, Fire, Water and Earth be balanced so that I can receive tomorrow...."

"All I need for perfect physical health...."

Be specific for any health areas.

My emotions; *"I need...relationship, etc."*

My business/my creative projects; *"I need...."*

Put your heart to work overnight on these manifestations.

The next day, observe the synchronicities. Time will speed up, things happen quickly.

The heart has many secrets and the secret language of your heart reveals itself slowly.

Imagine now, your heart's elements; Air, Fire, Water and Earth.

The Element of Air: is the first quarter of your heart/the left side of your heart/ the *Eastern Quarter*.

The Element of Fire: is the second quarter of your heart/at the bottom of your heart/the *Southern Quarter*.

The Element of Water: is the third quarter of your heart/the right side of your heart/the *Western Quarter*.

The Element of Earth: is the fourth quarter of your heart/at the top of your heart/the *Northern Quarter*.

Now imagine these four Elements of your heart having Masculine and Feminine quarters.

The Masculine Quarters are Air and Fire. The Feminine Quarters are Water and Earth.

The Masculine Quarters are on the left side of your heart and the Feminine Quarters are on the right side of your heart.

Notice that the Masculine Elements are on the left side of the heart, in polarity with The Feminine left side of the body; and the Feminine Elements are on the right side of the heart, in polarity with The Masculine right side of the body.

Now imagine looking at your heart or as a witness you can feel it as well. Which side or quarter feels dominant? It is the Air and Fire? Or Water and Earth? Allow yourself to just gently receive from the elements. For example: if the element of Fire seems strong, you may observe it being calmed by inviting the other elements to balance it out. If an element is unbalanced, you can feel the opposing element receiving or giving energy. We can balance our elements, bringing restored energy, life force and rejuvenation instantly.

We can support our heart's health at every level, by working or balancing the Masculine and Feminine elements bringing harmony to the heart. When the heart is harmonious, homeostasis is restored in the whole endocrine system. Peace and light are created. Life force returns and decisions can be made from a heart filled with peace.

The third law is: Frequency

The frequency of "All" brings the heart's secrets closer to you. When you call for the "All," you create with the "All." "All" brings the sum total of the cellular remembering. You are activating your cellular remembering when you bring to your heart its "All." All creation. All creation starts with the heart's remembering.

Creation can be activated through the heart's remembering. Your ability to create in this remembering brings you now into the power and mystery of creation. You are opening up to this creation now, as you birth your identity in this power vortex. You are flowing in this remembering now, as you begin the journey to the heart of all you ever were. Flowing in the remembering allows the essence; energy and life force to bring you all you need to receive love.

You are finding now a sense of new identity, suddenly; "you" have an identity. Your identity is your consciousness directed toward the heart. The heart remembers all. The heart feels all and the sheer enormity of being witness to this spectacle can leave you speechless. What a shock to discover the sunken treasure right in your garden, when you have searched throughout the ages and eons looking for it in someone else or something else.

Suddenly the shock can be overwhelming and there is a sense of displacement of you in your material world. The search is over. There is a sunken treasure, as you open its contents and discover its secrets; you weep at the enormity of whom "you" are. Look at me; I am just so unbelievable, just feeling this now, brings you a sense of pure peace; maybe for the first time in your life.

Carmel Glenane

You have in your hands and in your heart, your own "blue print" for yourself to step into the brave new frontier of "Self Responsibility" by listening to your "Secret Heart."

Heart I love you,

Carmel

Bibliography

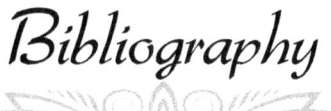

ALLEN, T. G.
The book of the dead
In-text: (Allen 1974)
Allen, Thomas George. 1974. *The Book Of The Dead*. Chicago: Oriental Institute of the University of Chicago.

BURNETT, F. H.
Secret Garden, The
In-text: (Burnett 2000)
Burnett, Frances Hodgson. 2000. *Secret Garden, The*. South Bend: Infomotions, Inc.

CALLEROS, M. A.V.
The Sacred Knowledge of the Maya
In-text: (Calleros 2011)
Calleros, M. A.V. 2011. *The Sacred Knowledge Of The Maya*. Miguel Calleros.

GERBER, R.
A practical guide to vibrational medicine
In-text: (Gerber 2001)
Gerber, Richard. 2001. *A Practical Guide To Vibrational Medicine*. New York, NY: Quill.

GLENANE, C.
The Alchemies of Isis Embodiment through The High Priestess
In-text: (Glenane 2016)
Glenane, C. 2016. *The Alchemies of Isis Embodiment through The*

High Priestess.
Littleton, CO.: Big Country Publishing, LLC

GLENANE, C.
Awaken your Immortal Intelligent Heart A Blue Print for Living in the Now.
In-text: (Glenane 2016)
Glenane, C. 2016. *Awaken your Immortal Intelligent Heart A Blue Print for Living in the Now.*
Littleton, CO.: Big Country Publishing, LLC

GLENANE, C.
Embodying The Divine Masculine of All Truth through The High Priest
In-text: (Glenane 2016)
Glenane, C. 2016. *Embodying The Divine Masculine of All Truth through The High Truth.*
Littleton, CO.: Big Country Publishing, LLC

HAWKINS, D. R.
Power vs. force
In-text: (Hawkins)
Hawkins, David R. *Power Vs. Force.*

MASTERS, R.
The Goddess Sekhmet
In-text: (Masters 2010)
Masters, Robert. 2010. The Goddess Sekhmet.
Ashland: White Cloud Press.

TEMPLE, R. K. G. AND TEMPLE, O.
The Sphinx mystery
In-text: (Temple and Temple 2009)
Temple, Robert K. G and Olivia Temple. 2009. *The Sphinx Mystery.*
Rochester, Vt.: Inner Traditions.

About The Author

Carmel Glenane B.A. Dip Ed. Owner/ Director of Atlantis Rising Healing Center™ and Mystery School. Founder of the philosophy of The Divine Feminine in 2002 and Senju Kannon™ Reiki in 2008, teaches The Divine Feminine Mysteries through her Mystery School Ascension Training program. A powerful interactive and dynamic motivational speaker, channelled writer, esoteric teacher, and sought-after healer, Carmel is known for her transformative tours to sacred destinations such as Hawaii, North, Central and South America, Turkey, India, Bali, Japan, Egypt and the great central heart of Australia, Uluru. With more than 20 years in business in personal development, Carmel's intent is to allow people to receive through the Heart's Intelligence through the mother's wisdom.

Carmel is the Australian Ambassador for HappyCharity.org as Director of Happy Spirits. She is currently writing training programs for all of her books to offer her courses online to a worldwide audience.

Feminine energy teaching programs became a focus after 10 years of founding my business Atlantis Rising Healing Centre in 1992, which led me to spontaneously become a channel for "The Goddess of All Light," who guided me to establish "The Philosophy of The Divine Feminine" in 2001. Daily my consciousness is aligned to "The Goddess of All Light," where I receive written transmissions for my personal guidance and teaching.

Carmel Glenane

Facilitating and leading my first teaching tour to Egypt in 2002; I have since taught in Egypt every year, as well as North, Central, and South America, Turkey, Greece, Hawaii Islands, Indonesia, India, and Australia. Each tour, book, and training has helped me "Earth" my body of Light; purging Earth attachments, as my ability to "Earth" (plug in) develops, holding more energy and light in my heart, for The Divine Ones to manifest.

In 2014, I was invited to open a Crystal Tones® Crystal Singing Bowl Sound Temple, and now incorporate these sonic Masterpieces into all my teaching programs.

I am in service to "The mother" and aim to have as many people as possible embody the teachings of our "Mother" through my books, teaching, and healing programs.

I am currently writing online courses to support The Atlantis Rising Mystery School ascension training program and creating new Guided Meditation mp3's to support the Ascension program.

To Connect with Carmel Glenane:
www.carmelglenane.com
www.senjukannonreiki.com
www.atlantis-rising.com.au
Ph: (+61) 0755 367 399

Recorded Meditations
By Carmel Glenane
featuring Crystal Tones Crystal Singing Bowls

New Dawn Meditation
By Carmel Glenane
Feat. Crystal Tones® Singing Bowls

Set Yourself Free Meditation
By Carmel Glenane
Feat. Crystal Tones® Singing Bowls

Core Identity Meditation
By Carmel Glenane
Feat. Crystal Tones® Singing Bowls

Carmel Glenane

Today I am Receiving Love
By Carmel Glenane
Feat. Crystal Tones® Singing Bowls

Trusting to Receive Love
By Carmel Glenane
Feat. Crystal Tones® Singing Bowls

The Alchemies of Isis The Magician Meditations
By Carmel Glenane
Feat. Crystal Tones® Singing Bowls

Embodying The High Priestess Meditations
By Carmel Glenane
Feat. Crystal Tones® Singing Bowls

The Immortals Meditations
By Carmel Glenane
Feat. Crystal Tones® Singing Bowls

Awakening The Intelligent Heart Meditations

By Carmel Glenane

Feat. Crystal Tones® Singing Bowls

The High Priest Meditations

By Carmel Glenane

Feat. Crystal Tones® Singing Bowls

The Miracle of The Mysteries Meditations

By Carmel Glenane

Feat. Crystal Tones® Singing Bowls

Embodying All Truth Meditations

By Carmel Glenane

Feat. Crystal Tones® Singing Bowls

All meditations are available on these and other fine retailers:

Other Books By Carmel Glenane

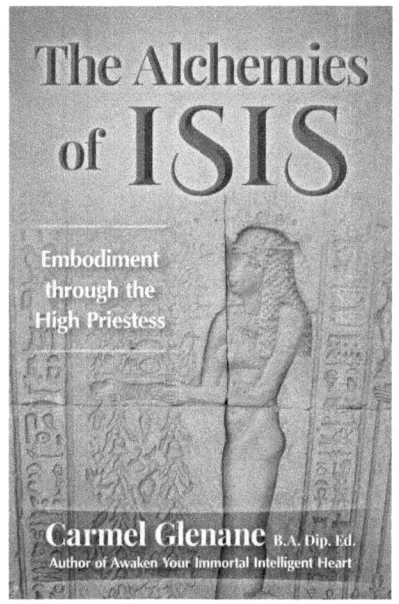

The Alchemies of Isis, Embodiment through the High Priestess By Carmel Glenane B.A. Dip. Ed.

Love fearlessly and passionately, for Love is timeless, infinite and unconditional!

Explore the Feminine energies with Isis and The High Priestess.

Carmel Glenane B.A.Dip.Ed. Author of several books on The Divine Feminine Mysteries has now combined *The Alchemies of Isis* with *The High Priestess* bringing readers the opportunity to embrace the secret wisdom of The Divine Feminine.

The *Isis* story is the story of all who love. Hope, restoration, and magic are yours when you lovingly embrace Isis in all her aspects. Every word brings Isis into your heart with "her" words of wisdom, power, truth and magic. Isis heals, restores, renews and resurrects new life; helping you open your heart to receive more love.

Carmel Glenane

In the companion volume *The High Priestess* Carmel explores core issues in women's lives; relationships, intimacy, emotional love and spirituality in direct dialogue with *The High Priestess*.

You will receive Moon, Stellar (star), Nature Speak Meditations and Rituals for activating your 'Core Identity' to receive love, as well as lessons inviting you to deepen your relationship with your heart's truth.

"The Alchemies of Isis teaches us that every woman needs to be grounded and feel empowered, to be truly sexy and secure. I now feel both."

Dr Shelley Sykes
TV Host and award-winning author of Sexy Single and Ready to Mingle.

Awaken Your Immortal Intelligent Heart, A Blue Print for Living in The Now **By Carmel Glenane B.A. Dip. Ed.**

ISBN: 978-1-938487-23-1 (print)
ISBN: 78-1-938487-24-8 (eBook)

In Part I: DISCOVER THE SECRET POWER OF YOUR HEART'S INTELLIGENCE

New scientific evidence reveals that your heart has an important role in supporting the Endocrine function of the entire human body. Read more as Glenane explores spiritually and scientifically the heart's important role in activating the Mitochondrial DNA (MtDNA). Discover how your heart's intelligence can be activated by initiating your five primary senses. Learn how The Black Heart, brings primordial power, pure peace and acceptance of all there is.

If you have a heart, you must read, "Awakening Your Immortal Intelligent Heart"

"Carmel Glenane does a magnificent job to remind the world that the center of our life is found by living from the center of our heart. In a time where consciousness is often mistaken for the mind, or even brain activity, Glenane presents a daily practice of heart-centered healing where weaving science, ancient spiritual disciplines, wisdom studies, and exercises of activation, provides the reader direct access to deep, personal growth. "
~*Brenda Littleton, M.A. Ed., M.A*

In Part II: THE IMMORTAL WOMAN

'The Immortal Woman' can be read sequentially or by opening up to any page for her message to be reflected upon for your day and see what 'She' reveals to you for your journey right now. Close your eyes, take a deep breath in, ask your question, then open the book up to a page. This book is your personal 'living guide' as the ancient secrets are revealed to you day by day. *'The Immortal Woman'* tests and challenges your previously held definition of Love and takes you to a space of truth for yourself where all of life becomes a multi-dimensional experience.

The Miracle of Mysteries Revealed through the Hearts Secrets

Embodying The Divine Masculine of All Truth Through The High Priest
By Carmel Glenane B.A. Dip. Ed.

ISBN: 978-1-938487-25-5 (print)
ISBN: 978-1-938487-26-2 (eBook)

Feel worthy to become a modern spiritual warrior seeking truth and creating a powerful new reality in your life!

- Are you ready to be a force of truth in our world?
- Why would your human journey not want a truth-filled experience?
- Do you give power and discipline to everything in your life?
- Are you worthy to become a modern spiritual warrior?
- Are you ready to activate your heart's intelligence?
- Are you ready to release your attachments?
- Are you willing to really manifest and rip out your illusions about your creative masculine?

Have you ever felt powerless in situations, relationships, etc.? All Truth teaches you to give power back to yourself when you are fearful. In Part I: All Truth brings ancient sacred laws to you and these laws are invisible forces that bring power to your whole totality. Feeling this now brings you closer to the essence and heart of yourself.

In Part II: Carmel Glenane, The High Priest, helps you explore and take control of your creative masculine. The High Priest offers a practical guide to living powerfully, with truth, changing your definition of your current reality. Explore your creative masculine and discover your power.

Allow yourself your truth through power
to bring protection, power and love!

Carmel Glenane Training and Workshop Programs

Carmel offers training and workshop programs on the Activation of The Intelligent Heart in Australia and overseas.

Training programs are also offered for all levels of Senju Kannon Reiki™, through the Atlantis Rising Mystery School.

Carmel also facilitates tours to sacred destinations throughout the world. Carmel travels with Crystal Tones Singing Bowls and invites you to bring your own bowl to be a witness to your heart's remembering in all sacred sites.

Carmel Glenane

If you wish to sponsor training programs please contact
the Atlantis Rising Healing Centre™ office:
email info@atlantis-rising.com.au

For upcoming workshops or training locations or tour destinations
please see our Website:
www.carmelglenane.com or www.atlantis-rising.com.au

Transformational Tours
Carmel Glenane Tour Facilitator

EGYPT TOURS

The essence of Egypt is in aligning your consciousness to the Ancient Deities themselves. The Hieroglyphics of the temples reflect, through the reliefs, architecture and atmosphere the energies of the Goddess's & Gods.

Egypt feeds your soul. Imagine being initiated to the frequencies in the Kings, Queens, and Subterranean chambers also known as the Pit in the Pyramid of Giza. Reflect on the timeless wonder of the Sphinx, touching the stele at the heart of its initiation chamber between the paws.

Discover old Atlantis again at Sakkara, as the desert winds whisper their secrets. Horus the Falcon hovers as he guides you to his temple complex in Edfu, revealing the essence of order, protection, and freedom — the ancient Egyptians were known for creating order out of chaos. Float upon the Nile, which reflects the starry body of the Goddess Nuit. Re-code your cellular memory with The Great Father Osiris as he resurrects your weary spirit in this most ancient of temples complexes in Abydos, healing you by the green Osirian well, where the secrets of the Ancient Flower of Life can be revealed. Be drawn to the mighty temple complex of Abu Simbel where Ramses II and Nefertari's love was immortalized.

Allow our holy Mother Isis to enfold you in her wings of love as we sail to her sacred home on The Isle of Philae.

The magician High Priestesses and Priests of Karnak allow you to embrace your own magical powers in their home of balance and duality. Sekhmet the austere warrior goddess/mother of Karnak will receive you if you respect her power.

Explore where ancient rituals and offerings were given to the stellar forces at Dendara, home of the Hathors, Goddesses of Love and Pleasure.

The Miracle of Mysteries Revealed through the Hearts Secrets

JAPAN TOURS

Japan is a transformational, feminine and nurturing experience, especially Mt. Kurama known as the 'heart' of Japan. Mt Kurama, located 40mins outside the imperial ancient city of Kyoto, is the mountain where Dr. USUI received his enlightenment. Japan's delicate and very special spiritual energies reflect the beauty and power of Senju Kannon Mother of Japan and mother of our Feminine Reiki.

The Japan journey begins in the ancient shrine city of Kyoto, visiting powerful Buddhist temples, including Sanjusangen-do–The Thousand Armed Kannon Temple with 1,000 Kannon's (also known as Quan Yin) statues in the temple. The city's beauty is phenomena, featuring spectacular gardens, a geisha district, authentic Japanese cuisine, peace, order and tranquility. Unwind in traditional Onsen style bathing houses of warm mineral springs, relax in the peaceful retreat rooms or indulge in authentic traditional Japanese cuisine.

Our training program honors the Dr. Usui (traditional Reiki) but embraces 'The Mother' feminine heart of Reiki. Our programs are tailored to sacred sites and locations in and around the Temples at Kyoto and Mr Kurama. Travelling with our Crystal Tones Singing bowls magnifying and amplifying this incredible energy.

www.ingramcontent.com/pod-product-compliance
Lightning Source LLC
Chambersburg PA
CBHW071631080526
44588CB00010B/1355